AIDAN m. A de_____e.'' There are at least twenty _____me—Saint Aidan of Iona is the most famous. He established a renowned monastery on the island of Lindisfarne off the north coast of Britain, where he sought to Christianize the pagan Saxons.

BRIGID/Brighid f. A goddess revered throughout the Celtic world, Brighid (breed) is a divinity associated with fire, agriculture, and poetry. The most well-known saint by this name is Saint Brigid of Kildare, who in folklore seems to have taken on many of the properties and powers of her older pagan namesake. The name became wildly popular in the eighteenth century, eventually being used as a generic name for an Irish woman.

COREY m. In Ireland, this name is thought to have derived from a variety of surnames that include the root *corra*, ''spear.'' Though rarely used as a first name there, it became popular in the United States as a boy's name, especially in the 1960s.

KIERAN m. (c'iar-on) Although there were twenty-six saints in Ireland with this name, it didn't find favor as a secular name in Ireland until around the 1950s. Saint Ciaran of Clonmacnoise was the founder of a famous monastery in the sixth century, which remained an important religious center through to the sixteenth century.

LIAM m. This is the more popular Irish form of the Germanic name William, a compound name meaning ''will helmet.'' Uilliam is the older, more formal Irish translation, but Liam is much more widely used, currently gaining popularity in the United States and recently figuring in the top ten selected names for boys in Britain.

SINEAD/Sinéad f. (shin-ade) An Irish form of the name Jane, or more properly, Janet, which are feminine forms derived from John. John was hugely popular as a man's name from the Middle Ages on, and Christians throughout Europe developed feminine versions. The name is presently popular in Ireland, and has become more familiar internationally in the past twenty years. Sinéidín (shin-aideen) is a pet form.

O'Baby

The Irish Baby Name Book

GEOFFREY JOHNSON

BERKLEY BOOKS, NEW YORK

O'BABY: THE IRISH BABY NAME BOOK

A Berkley Book / published by arrangement with
the author

PRINTING HISTORY
Berkley edition / April 1999

For information address: The Berkley Publishing Group,
a member of Penguin Putnam Inc.,
375 Hudson Street, New York, New York 10014.

The Penguin Putnam Inc. World Wide Web site address is
http://www.penguinputnam.com

ISBN: 0-425-16818-2

BERKLEY®
Berkley Books are published by The Berkley Publishing Group,
a member of Penguin Putnam Inc., 375 Hudson Street,
New York, New York 10014.
BERKLEY and the "B" design
are trademarks belonging to Berkley Publishing Corporation.

PRINTED IN THE UNITED STATES OF AMERICA

10 9 8 7 6 5 4 3 2 1

Contents

Introduction

§ It is not entirely remarkable that Irish names have taken on widespread usage throughout the English-speaking world. The Irish themselves have spread to every corner of that world, and indeed, farther afield. It was inevitable that the impact of their culture would be felt wherever they settled and prospered. Today, some Irish names enjoy such commonplace usage as to have almost broken free from their original sources: Brian, for instance, or Sheila. Quite recently, Kevin emerged as the most popular chosen boy's name in France. In the United Kingdom, the names Ryan and Liam placed in the top ten favored names for boys in 1996. Connor placed thirteenth that year, and the names Kieran and Sean also figured within the top fifty favorites. In the United States Brandon, Ryan, and Cody all feature in the top twenty most popular names for boys in recent years. A little farther down the list, Irish stalwarts Brian, Patrick, Sean, and Connor appear within the top fifty.

Patrick is, surprisingly, back in favor in Ireland in recent years. Perhaps that period when it fell from grace, being too much the national name, too frequently found among a generation, has passed, and it has a fresh appeal to present-day parents. In Ireland itself, use of Irish names had fallen as low as a mere 20 percent for boys and 8 percent for girls at the beginning of this century. Today, up to 40 percent of boys' first names in Ireland derive from Irish forms. Eoin, Rory, Ryan, Niall, Conor, Sean, and Cian are well-represented among the current favorite selections.

In common with other nationalities, Irish parents seem more reluctant to experiment with male names than with female names. Girls' names have traditionally always been more foreign, original, and imaginative in their makeup. And while use of Irish names for girls is well up since the beginning of the century, only one name, Aoife, currently makes the top ten list of preferred girls' names in Ireland.

In the United Kingdom, the situation for Irish girls' names is similar, with Shannon placing highest in recent years, just outside the top ten. A little farther down the list, Molly, with its distinctive Irish accent, occurs.

Molly has begun a slow, steady rise in the United States also, though it trails behind the more established favorites Caitlin, Kelly, and Shannon. The highest-ranked Irish girls' names in the United States figure as the freely spelled variants of older names: Katelyn, Kaitlyn, and Brianna all figure among the top fifty, along with the more traditional Erin. Kayla, placed at number ten, is perhaps currently the most popular girl's name with an Irish lilt.

Trends, however, are mercilessly—or perhaps mercifully— brief. Once a name becomes recognized as commonplace, it experiences a sharp decline in adoption. With this maxim in mind, this book hopes to present a broad variety of alternatives. Of course, some of these names will not be used again, but something may be learned of the practice of name-making and name-giving through acquaintance with the names presented here, many of which are more than a thousand years old. The persistent popular use of biblical names is adequate testament to the agelessness of certain forms. As cultures strive toward greater self-awareness, name-giving and name-making reflect this process. Some names endure, some die out. Some disappear for a while and are later reborn. In Ireland itself, the reawakening of interest in older Irish traditions coupled with a growing self-confidence with regard to place in an expanding global community offers more occasion than ever for people to come into contact with traditional and more recent Irish names. This makes for more occasions for people to wonder about the origins, meanings, and sounds of these names. Some answers lie within. Ultimately it is hoped that the reader will find at least one name here, which will not continue to live merely within the pages of this book.

Little Dark One

There is evidence to suggest that settlers arrived in Ireland as early as 3500 B.C. What little is known about these peoples derives from the megalithic tombs they left throughout the country. Many of these sites show evidence of highly civilized communities with complex knowledge of astronomical and architectural principles. But who these peoples were and how they lived remain topics for speculation. It is probable that over the following 3,000 years, there occurred regular invasions and incursions of new settlers, each leaving their mark on the societies they challenged. It is with the arrival of the Celts, about 600 B.C., that our picture of early Irish history becomes more clear.

The Celts are thought to have come to Ireland in four major waves. Originally coming out of what is now known as the Middle East, they spread westward and northward across Europe. The earliest arrivals to Ireland were known as the Pretani or Cruithnigh (crthnew) and are thought to have arrived in the north of the country via Scotland. Later followed the Euerni or Érainn (from whence the evolution of the country name Éire), also known as the Fir Bolg, and

then the Laighin, who gave their name to the province of
Leinster. The last major Celtic influx occurred around 50
B.C., and these people rose eventually to dominate the pre-
ceeding tribes. They were known as the Gaeil.

There is some archaeological evidence to suggest that the
Gaeil came out of Spain, and it is likely that in physical
character they may have shared similarities with current natives of northern Spain, being typically dark-haired and pale-
skinned. A seventeenth-century geneaologist, Dubaltach Mac
Firbhisigh (dualtach mac firvisi) records, "Everyone who is
fair-skinned, brown-haired, bold, honourable and daring . . .
is of the true Gaeil." The meaning of Dubaltach's name—
however, with its suggestion of swarthy coloring—may have
aligned him more typically with the earlier settlers, the Fir
Bolg, peoples he unfortunately holds in low contempt:"Everyone who is black-haired, vociferous, ill-doing, tale-telling,
vulgar, stingy and mean . . . is of the Fir Bolg."

Being that as it may, there exists a distinctive group of
names, in use from earliest times on, that proudly proclaim
dark coloring as a mark of honor and respect. Here are some
notable instances.

BARRDHUBH f. (bar-uv) "dark-headed, dark-haired." A
name with regal associations in both Ulster and Clones.

BRANDUBH/Branduff m. (bran-duv) "raven-black." A
name relatively common in early Ireland, borne by, among
others, a king of Leinster, two saints, and, indeed, an ancient
board game.

CIARA/Ciar/Cioara/Ciarra/Keara/Kiera/Kira f. (k'iar-a)
"dark, black." A modern form of the old Irish name Ciar,
itself a feminine form of Kieran. A recent strong resurgence
brought Ciara to the forefront as the most popular Irish girl's

name chosen in Ireland in 1990. Saint Ciara of Kilkeary, County Tipperary, was a distinguished seventh-century figure who established two monasteries.

CIARMHAC m. (k'iar-vok) "dark son." An unusual name from the south that has given rise to the Munster surname of Kirby (O Ciarmhaic).

CIARNAIT f. (k'iar-nit) "dark lady." Another feminine form of the name Kieran. Ciarnait was mistress to King Cormac Mac Art of Tara.

CRÓNÁN/Cronan m. (kron-awn) "swarthy, sallow, dark-skinned" or "brown one." A number of saints bore this name, the most famous, Saint Cronan of Roscrea. Croney and Cronin are other forms.

DARCY f. & m. In Ireland, a name from the surname O Dorchaidhe, "descendant of the dark one." Used commonly today in America as a girl's name, but previously given to boys as well. Other forms are Darcey, Darcie, Darci, and Dorcy.

DONAGH/Donncha/Donnchadh m. (dun-a) "brown warrior." A common name in late medieval times, with usage by kings and princes recorded, notably in the personage of the son of Brian Boru. Anglicized in time variously as Denis, Dionysius, Donat, Donatus, Donogh, and Donaghy, it is equivalent with the Scottish name Duncan.

DONEGAN/Donnagan m. Use of the surname as a first name. Donnagan is a pet form of Donn.

DONLA/Dúnlaith f. "brown lady" or "lady of the *dun* (fortress)." A name with a record of royal usage, popular in the early Middle Ages. May be Anglicized as Dunla.

DONLEAVY/Doinnlé/Donn Slébe m. "brown one of the mountain." Found more usually as a last name in Ireland today.

DONN m. (dun, or down) "brown." Donn was the god of the dead in Irish mythology, a fact that did not seem to dissuade popular use of the name in the Middle Ages. "Tech Duinn," Donn's house, was the Otherworld.

DONNÁN m. (dun-awn) "little brown one." A diminutive of Donn. A name recorded as that of four saints.

DONOVAN/Donnabhán m. "dark brown, swarthy person." A name coming principally from the south, more usually a last name in Ireland today. May be rendered as Donavan or Donavon.

DOUGAL/Dubhghall/Dubgall m. "dark foreigner." One of the names given to the invading Vikings, probably used for the darker-haired Danes. The name was used mostly in the north and in Scotland, where it is still popular today.

DOUGLAS/Dubhglas m. Compound of *dubh*, "black" and *glas*, "green, blue, gray." More in use in Scotland, this Gaelic name was a common title for rivers and may have been used to denote someone who lived near a river.

DOYLE m. Use of the surname as a first name. Doyle derives from O Dubhghaill (O'Doyle), "descendant of Dougal."

DUALTACH/Dubaltach/Dubhaltach m. (doo-al-tach) "black jointed, dark-limbed." A name common in medieval times and borne by a distinguished seventeenth-century historian, Dubaltach Mac Firbhisigh. Anglicized as Dualta or Duald.

DUANE m. A contemporary use of the surname as a first name. From O Dubain, "descendant of the dark (-haired) one." Popularly rendered Dwane or Dwayne, and also as Dwain, Dwaine, and recently, DeWayne.

DUBH m. (duv) "black, dark." Anglicized as Duff, now usually found as a surname in Ireland and Scotland, but also used as a first name in this form.

DUBHAGÁN/Dubacán m. (doo-gan) From *dub*, "dark, black" or "little dark lad." Anglicized Duggan or Doogan.

DUBHÁN/Dubán m. (doo-an) "dark (-haired) person." A name borne by two saints, and which gave rise to the surname O Dubain, and hence Duane.

DUBHDALEITHE/Dub Dá Leithe m. (doo-daw-le-he) "dark man of the two sides." Enough said. An early name with quite a common usage. Anglicized as Dudley.

DUBHDARA/Dubhdarach m. (doo-dara) "dark man of the oak." A name from west Connacht.

DUBHÓG f. & m. (duv-ogue) "little dark one."

DUBHTHACH/Dubthach/Dufach f. & m. (doo-fach) "dark one." A frequent early name that legend says was borne by the father of Saint Brigid.

DUIBHEASA/Dubh Easa/Duvessa f. (div-as-a) "dark lady of the waterfall." A name from the Middle Ages, associated with the O'Donoghues of Killarney.

DUIBHLEAMHNA/Dub Lemna f. (div-lown-a) "dark lady of Lemain." A royal name from the tenth century.

DUINNSECH f. (doon-shock) "brown-haired girl."

FEARDORCHA/Ferdorcha m. (far-dur-eka) "dark man." A name in frequent use throughout the sixteenth century, Latinized as Obscurus. In Donegal, it has been shortened to Dorrie.

GORMÁN f. & m. (gurm-awn) "dark, swarthy." A name borne by, among others, a king of Munster, Gorman Mac Airtri, ancestor of the O'Keefes.

KERRY f. & m. A name taken from the county name in Ireland. In Irish, Ciarraí, "land of the descendants of Ciar." In this instance the Ciar referred to the son of the legendary queen Maeve. The name was used popularly for boys in Australia but has since been used more frequently for girls in the United States and Britain. Kerrie, Keri, Kerri, and Keree are other forms.

KERWIN m. "descendant of the dark, black one." From the Irish surname O Ciardhubháin. Uncommon in Ireland. Also found as Kerwinn, Kerwaine, Kervin, and Kervyn.

KIERAN/Ciaran/Ciarán/Kieron/Kyran m. (c'iar-on) From *ciar,* "dark" or "black." A name that has become widely popular abroad, as well as in Ireland. Despite the fact that records show there were some twenty-six saints in Ireland with this name, it did not find favor as a secular name in Ireland until around the 1950s, and then in the Anglicized form, Kieran, the most frequently used form today. Saint Ciaran of Clonmacnoise was the founder of a famous monastery in the sixth century, which remained an important religious center through to the sixteenth century.

ODHAR m. (or) A name meaning "gray-brown, dark sallow," or possibly the old word for an otter.

ORAN/Odhran/Órán m. From the name Odhar, "gray-brown." Some seventeen saints are recorded with this name, one of whom, according to tradition, was brother of Saint Ciaran of Clonmacnoise. In legend, Odhran was the charioteer of Saint Patrick. The name has been used widely in the United States, where it has been rendered variously as Orin(n), Orran, and Or(r)en. In literature, writers Eugene O'Neill and Raymond Chandler have made use of the name.

ORNA/Odharnait/Órnait f. The female form of Oran. The name of a virgin saint venerated on November 13, about whom little is known.

TEIMHNÍN (t'ein-een) m. From *temen*, "dark." A name borne by two saints, and possibly the source of the contemporary surname Tynan.

The Fairest of Them All

§ Fair hair was less characteristic of the early Irish and, predictably, it became a mark of special distinction. Brightness of hair and skin was very much part of the ancient Irish ideal of beauty in both men and women. To Dubaltach Mac Firbhisigh, such coloration was enough to denote descent from the race of mythical deities believed to have been the original inhabitants of Ireland: the Tuatha Dé Danann, "people of Dana." "Everyone who is fair-haired, honorable, tall and musical . . . is of the Tuatha Dé Danann." Fairy and Otherworld figures are frequently described as having lustrous golden or silver-colored hair. With the coming of the Vikings, ruthless invaders from the Scandinavian countries, the Irish learned to be a little less starry-eyed about such appearances. The use of names that praised fair coloring persisted, nevertheless, perhaps with regard to the heroic ages from whence many of them originated. The following is a sample of such names, all jostling to better the claims of the other and be "the fairest of them all."

ALBANY f. & m. The poetic name for Scotland, or Scotland and England, derived from the old Irish name Alba, which is thought to have connections with the root *albino*, "white."

ALBY/Ailbhe/Ailbe f. & m. Probably derived from a word for "white." The name Ailbhe occurs frequently in Irish legend, most famously in the person of Ailbhe Gruadbrecc ("of the freckled cheeks"), daughter of Cormac Mac Art, and favorite of Finn Mac Cool. She is celebrated as being one of the four best women of her time. Saint Ailbhe of Tipperary, a contemporary of Saint Patrick, is a famous male bearer of the name. Alvy, Elva, and Oilbhe are other recorded forms.

BÁINE f. (bawn-e) "whiteness, paleness." An early name occurring in legend.

BARRFIND/Bairrfhionn f. & m. (barrin) "fair-headed, fair-haired." A name borne by eight saints, one of whom was a woman. Barra, Bairre, and Barre are pet forms, but the Anglicized Barry is the most popularly used form.

BARRY m. This is the Anglicized form of the pet names Barra and Bairre, which derive from Barrfind and Finbarr. Barry has been used also to Anglicize the name Bearach. In the twentieth century it quite sweepingly supplanted all its connected forms in Ireland and Britain and became especially successful in Australia, where it has been shortened to Baz and Bazza, and where, along with Bruce, it is now considered generic.

BEVIN/Béibhinn/Bébinn f. "white lady, fair lady." Béibhinn was a very popular name in early Ireland. In legend, Béibhinn appears as a golden-haired giantess who flees her

giant husband, Aodh Álainn ("the beautiful"), and seeks
sanctuary with Finn Mac Cool. In the past, the name was
spuriously Anglicized as Vivian.

CAOIMHINN f. (keev-in) "beautiful and fair." An early
name borne by, among others, one of the ancestors of the
O'Briens. For those daunted by the Gaelic spelling, Keevin
might be an acceptable Anglicization.

CÉIBHIONN f. (kayv-un) "lady of fair locks." A mythological name.

FINBARR/Finnbarr/Fionbharr m. A name composited
from the same elements as Barrfind, "fair-topped, fair-
haired." In folktales, Finbarr is the leader of the fairy host.
The name was also borne by eight saints, the most important
of whom is a patron saint of Cork and about whom many
miraculous stories exist. A popular name today in Ireland, it
is sometimes shortened to Barra, Bairre, or Barry.

FINN/Fionn m. "fair, brilliant white, light-hued." Finn was
the name of several legendary heroes, the most important of
whom, Finn Mac Cool (Fionn Mac Cumaill), is a central
figure in Irish folklore and mythology. He was a renowned
warrior, wise, brave, and handsome. The Fianna, the king's
bodyguard, which he captained, were named for him. Many
heroic and magical tales exist about the deeds of Finn and
his warriors, and he is essentially identified with a heroic age
in Ireland. He was father to Oisín, and later the scourge of
Dermot and Grainne. In the twentieth century, writers James
Joyce in *Finnegans Wake,* and Flann O'Brien in *At Swim
Two Birds*, have continued to use him as an inspirational
character. In recent times in the United States, the name has
been used also for girls.

FINNCHNEAS f. (fin-chnas) Literally, "fair-skin." Quite a mouthful by today's standards, in legend Finnchneas was robe-maker to the Fianna.

FINNEACHT f. (fin-acht) A feminine derivation from Finn. The name of a virgin saint.

FINNÉADAN f. (fin-aiden) "fair brow."

FINNEGAN/Fionnagán m. A diminutive form of Finn.

FINNIAN/Finian/Finnén m. A name derived from the Irish name Finn, with a British element added. Some have suggested that Finnian is an early British form of Finbarr. Several Irish saints have borne the name, the most important of these, Finnian of Clonard, County Meath, and Finnian of Movill, County Down, both of whom spent time in Britain. In the twentieth century, the name took on renewed familiarity with the 1960s stage musical and film, *Finian's Rainbow*.

FINNSEACH f. (fin-sech or fin-she) "fair lady, blond girl." A name recorded as that of two saints.

FINOLA/Fionnuala/Fionnghuala f. "fair-shouldered, white shoulder." Fionnuala (fin-uala) was a very popular name during the Middle Ages in Ireland and is still widely used today in this, its Irish form, and in the Anglicized form, Finola. One Fionnuala was the mother of the sixteenth-century rebel chieftain Red Hugh O'Donnell, and is credited with being the driving force behind her son's illustrious career. Flora MacDonald (1722–1790), the Scottish heroine who aided the deposed Scottish regent Bonnie Prince Charlie (of "My Bonnie Lies Over the Ocean" fame), was likely another Fionnuala, or Fenella, the preferred Scottish form, Flora being then a standard Anglicization of the name. The shortened form Nuala, has been used since the thirteenth century and is still quite popular.

FINTAN/Fiontan m. Possibly "white fire" or "the white ancient." In mythology, Fintan was said to have lived for thousands of years. From ecclesiastical sources, there are no less than seventy-four saints recorded with this name. Still widely used in Ireland.

FIONNÚIR/Fionnabhair f. (fenoor) "white ghost" or "white sprite." Fionnúir was the daughter of Maeve, legendary queen of Connacht. High King Conor Mac Nessa also gave this name to his daughter. Fennore is a possible Anglicization.

KEELIN/Caoilfhionn f. A compound of *caol,* "slender," and *fionn,* "fair, white." The name is found as Caoilinn and Cáelinn as well in Ireland where, though consistently used, it rarely occurs in the English form, Keelin. The U.S. names Kaylyn and Kaelan may have some connection. Several saints of record have borne the name.

KELLY/Ceallach f. & m. Traditionally interpreted as meaning "frequenter of churches," recent opinion holds that this is a much older name meaning "bright-headed." Even in older days, the name was used for both girls and boys. Early records reveal a more frequent male usage of the name, but from the mid-twentieth century on, it has proven very popular as a girl's name in Britain, the United States, Canada, and Australia. Predictably, variable spellings occur, and it is likely that the popular names Keely and Kylie have some connection with this vogue. Interestingly enough, Kelly is once more finding favor as a boy's name in the United States.

LACHTNA m. (locht-na) "milklike, milk-colored." An early name from the south borne by an ancestor of Brian Boru. Lachtnán is a diminutive form from whence we get the surname Lawton.

MOINGIONN/Moingfhionn f. & m. (mong-in) "fair-haired." An early name borne by two princesses.

MUIREANN/Muirenn f. (mwi-ran) "sea white, sea fair." A popular early name occurring frequently in legend. Muireann was the wife of Oisín. It is found as Mairenn, Morinn and, in Icelandic texts, as Myrun.

MUIRGHEAL f. (mwir-ial) "sea bright." This is the Irish form of the widley used Celtic name, which is now Anglicized as Muriel. Three queens of record bore the name. Meryl and Meriel are related forms.

UAINIONN f. (oo-anin) "foam white."

Little Red One

§ The Irish are notoriously characterized as red-haired and pale-skinned, with a typical propensity toward freckles. Of course, this is merely a crude caricature—there are many more dark-haired than red-haired Irish—but this coloration must have been particularly distinctive to other races in earlier times. Early Irish names themselves display quite an appreciation of ruddy coloring in individuals. Parents of newly arrived red-haired children may find a suitable name to their liking among the following class of names. Indeed, regardless of coloring, many of the following names may be appealing. It is quite likely that these names were often applied without regard for description but as evocative titles or commemorations of earlier ancestors. Red as a color has obvious associations with warfare—another Celtic enthusiasm—and hence, kingship. Every parent knows they are in the presence of royalty alongside their newborn, and a name with regal connotations might be just the thing.

ÁDHAMH m. (awv) "red earth." A Gaelic translation of the biblical Adam.

BREAC m. (brack) "freckled, speckled." A popular name in early medieval times, especially in the south. Breacán is the diminutive.

BREACNAIT f. (beck-nit) "freckled girl." A feminine from Breac.

BRICÍN m. (brick-een) "little freckled one." Another diminutive form of Breac.

CLANCY f. & m. The contemporary surname used as a first name. It is an Anglicization of the Irish Mac Fhlannchadha, "son of the red warrior."

COCCÁN m. (kuk-awn) An early name probably meaning "red."

COCHRANN f. (kuch-ran) "red lady." Cochrann was the daughter of King Cathaoir Mór, and mother of the legendary Diarmait Ua Duibne, who eloped with Grainne.

CORC/Corcc m. (kurk) "red, crimson," but also possibly an older word meaning "heart." An early southern name, which appears in legendary tracts as well as in records from the later Middle Ages. Corcán is a diminutive.

CORCAIR/Corccair f. (kurk-ir) "red, crimson." The feminine form of Corc.

CORCRÁN m. (kurk-rawn) From *corcur,* "red, crimson, purple." The surname Corcoran derives from this name.

CRIOFAN/Crimthann/Criomthann m. (kree-fan) "a fox." A very popular medieval name, it is rarely encountered today as a first name. Various Anglicized forms have been Creon, Crehan, Criffin, Griffin, and Crevan.

DEARGÁN m. (dara-gawn) "little red one."

DERRY m. From the surname O Doireidh, "descendant of the red-haired one." Derry is also used popularly as a pet form of Dermot.

EARC/Erc f. & m. (ark) Meaning possibly "speckled, dark red" or "a salmon." This is an early name that had some popularity. In the mythic tales, Erc was a lady of the Fianna. There is a record of a Saint Erc, bishop of Slane.

EARCÁN m. (ark-awn) "little speckled one" or "little red one." A diminutive of Earc.

EARCNAIT/Ercnat f. (ark-nit) Feminine diminutive of Earc. Saint Earcnait was dressmaker and embroiderer to Saint Colmcille.

FLANN f. & m. (flan or flown) "bright red, bloodred." A very popular early name, records show use by kings, queens, poets, and saints. In the later Middle Ages the name was Latinized Florentius, and then Anglicized as Florence. In contemporary usage, the name is familiar from the writer Brian O'Nolan (1911–1966) who used the pen name Flann O'Brien.

FLANNAGAN/Flannacán m. A diminutive form of Flann, from which derives the surname O'Flannagan.

FLANNAIT f. (flon-it) Feminine form of Flannán. Saint Flannait was foundress of a church near Fermoy on the Blackwater.

FLANNÁN m. (flan-awn) "little bloodred one." A pet form of Flann. Saint Flannán of Killaloe gave his name to the outer Hebrides Islands, the Flannan Islands.

FLANNCHADH/Flannacha m. (flan-ach-a) "red warrior." From this name we get the surname Mac Fhlanncahdha, which has been Anglicized Clancy.

FLANNERY f. & m. Originating from a name meaning "red eyebrows." The surname used as a first name, popularly associated with the American Southern author, Flannery O'Connor.

FLYNN f. & m. The surname used as a first name. A derivation from Flann, "bright bloodred."

RORY m. From the Irish, Ruaidhrí, "red king, great king." An old and popular medieval name, Ruaidhrí was used by regal and nonregal personages. Rory O'Connor (Ruadrí Ua Conchobair), who died in 1198, was the last monarch to own the title High King of Ireland. In its contemporary Anglicized form, it is still popular in Ireland today.

ROWAN m. From the Irish name, Rúadhán, "red-haired."

RÚADHÁN/Ruan m. (ru-awn) "red-haired" or "little red-haired one." Saint Rúadhán of Lorrha, County Tipperary, from the sixth century, has many stories connected with him, in one of which he cursed the royal court at Tara, leading to its devastation. The Anglicized form is Rowan, distinct in origin from the feminine name connected with the mountain ash tree.

RÚADHNAIT f. (rue-nit) "red-haired girl," a feminine form of Rúadhán. In the legends of the saints, Saint Rúadhnait appears as sister to Saint Rúadhán of Lorrha.

RUAIDHRÍ/Ruairí/Ruadrí m. (rua-ree) "great king, red king." A name with a long pedigree among kings and commoners. In the course of its usage, it has been Anglicized Roderick, Roddy, Rhoddy, Roger, and Richard, but is most faithfully rendered as Rory.

Radiant Child

§ Most early civilizations have shown special homage to the sun and its properties of illumination and heat. Divinities associated with the sun rank high in importance. The Celtic settlers known as the Érainn later became known as the Fir Bolg, "men of Bolg." Bolg is the Irish form of the Celtic name Bolgi, the most widely used name among the Celts for the sun god. Light and brightness were equated with divinity, and in due course were invoked in the names people chose. The following group of names, many of them very early in origin, is a representation of this instinct to convey an aura of light and evoke the power and protection it could bring.

AIDAN/Áedán/Aodhán m. A derivative of Aodh. This form is a diminutive, meaning "little fire." Aidan is the popular Anglicized spelling of the older Irish forms, Áedán and Aodhán. In early usage, it was relatively common, with no less than twenty-one saints of record bearing the name. Saint Aidan of Iona is probably the most famous of these. He established a renowned monastery on the island of Lindisfarne off the north coast of Britain, from whence he sought to Christianize the pagan Saxons. Popular today, the name also has a history of usage in northern England. It has also been rendered Aiden and Aedan.

ÁINE f. (awn-ye) "radiance, splendor, brilliance." An ancient name, probably originally that of a divinity, it was used in earliest times by both men and women but since has only been used as a female name. There are many old stories of a goddess Áine and of fairy women of the same name. The kings of Munster claimed her as an ancestor, as did the later conquering Norman family the Fitzgeralds. In the Finn tales, Áine is one of the wives of Finn Mac Cool, Ireland's pre-eminent mythological hero figure. As a human figure, she appears as "the best-hearted woman who ever lived." The name was Anglicized as Ann(e), Anna, and Hannah, names with which it has no real connection.

AODH m. (ay) A name meaning "fire," very popular in early Ireland, and probably from a name for a god. Numerous kings and high kings bore the name, as well as the mythical figure Aodh Eangach who, it was prophesied, would arise as a champion of the people in a time of need, much like the legendary Arthur of Britain. Some twenty saints are recorded with this name. It was Anglicized as the unrelated Hugh, a name itself with famous national connotations in the figures of Hugh O'Neill (c.1540–1616) and Red Hugh O'Donnell (c.1571–1602), rebel leaders in the uprising against Elizabeth I. Aodhaigh (ay-hee) is a pet form, which has been equated with Hughey, a name still popular in the north.

AODHAGÁN m. (ay-gawn) Diminutive form of Aodh, hence, "little fire." Anglicized as Egan.

AODHAMAIR/Adamair f. (ay-amir or aid-emir) A feminine derivation from Aodh, "fire." In ecclesiastical legend, Aodhamair was the first woman to be made a nun by Saint Patrick.

AODHNAIT f. (ay-nit) A feminine diminutive of Aodh. Anglicized as Enat.

AOIBHEALL f. (ee-vell) "radiance, spark, fire." The name of an older Irish goddess. Associated with pagan times, it was also a name given to the fairy woman who appeared to High King Brian Boru on the eve of the battle of Clontarf.

AOIBHGRÉINE f. (eve-gren) "radiance of the sun, ray of sunshine." In legend Aoibhgréine was the daughter of the tragic lovers, Deirdre and Naoise. Evegren is an Anglicization and a much friendlier spelling.

AOIFE f. (ee-fah) "radiant, beautiful, pleasant." An early name, probably that of a goddess. The name appears in many old myths and folk stories, as well as in the historical personage of Aoife, daughter of Dermot, king of Leinster, who married Strongbow, leader of the invading Normans. Eva is an unrelated Anglicization. Presently very popular, in 1997, Aoife was the only Irish name to place in the top ten popular choices of girls' names in Ireland.

BEOAODH m. (byo-ay) "living fire." The name of a sixth-century saint.

DAIGH m. (dei) "flame, fire." A popular name in early Ireland. Saint Daigh was a sixth-century saint renowned for his skillful craftsmanship.

DAIGHRE m. (dei-re) "flame, fire." In legend, Daighre was a musician of the Fianna.

EAVAN/Aoibhinn/Aoibheann f. (even) "beautiful sheen, fair radiance." A name with royal associations in the tenth century, and the name of the mother of Saints Enda and Fainche. Eavan is the popular contemporary Anglicized spelling.

EAVNAT/Aoibhnait f. (eve-nit) "radiant girl." A derivation from Aoibhinn.

EIBHLEANN/Eibhliu f. (ev-len or ev-le) "sheen, beauty, radiance." An older Irish name, thought to have been that of a sun goddess. It is distinct from the similarly written Eibhlin, which is the Irish form of the Germanic name Eveline or Evelyn. Appropriate Anglicizations might be Evle or Evlin.

GORMLAITH f. (gurm-la) "illustrious princess, splendid lady." A very popular name in early Ireland, particularly among royalty. Many distinguished women have borne the name, some of them enjoying spectacular regal careers as they outlived their warlike spouses to remarry into second dynasties. One such was Gormlaith, daughter of the king of Leinster, who was first married to Olaf, the Viking leader of Dublin, by whom she bore Sitric, who would become known as Silkenbeard, a powerful Viking ruler in Dublin. She then married Malachy, the high king, and later, Brian Boru, scourge of the Vikings. Norse scribes refer to her as Kormlada and note she was "fairest and best-gifted in everything that was not in her own power, but it was the talk of men that she did all things ill over which she had any power." The name is found as Gormla, and might be Anglicized

Gormley. Peculiarly, the name has traditionally been equated with Barbara.

GRIAN f. (gree-an) "sun" or "sun goddess." Possibly a name for the sun goddess, Grian also appears in legend as the daughter of Finn Mac Cool.

KEEGAN m. The surname used as a first name. Derived from Mac Aodhagain, "son of Aodhagan." Also found as Keagan and Keegen.

LAISREÁN m. (loss-ran) A diminutive from *laisre,* "flame."

LAOISE f. (lee-sha) "radiant girl." Possibly a form of *Luighseach,* a feminine diminutive from the divine name Lugh, "light, brightness."

LASAIR f. (loss-ir) "flame, fire." A relatively common early name.

LASAIRÍONA/Lasairfhiona f. (loss-ir-ina) A compound of *lasair,* "flame," and *fion* "wine"; "fire of wine." A popular name in the later Middle Ages. Lassarina is an Anglo form.

LÓCH/Luach m. & f. (lowch) "bright, radiant." An old name with pagan associations. Diminutive forms are Lóchán and Luachán (low-chawn and lu-chawn).

LUGH m. (lu) "light, brightness." The name of a Celtic god, son of the goddess Eithne. Lugh was the patron of artists and craftsmen. Lughán (lu-awn) is a diminutive.

LUGHAIDH/Lúí m. (lu-ee) From Lugh. This was one of the most popular names in early Ireland, though rarely encountered today. Lewy, Lewis, Louis, and Aloysius are recorded Anglicizations.

MEALLA/Meall f. (mall-a, mall) From an old word for "lightning." In legend, Meall was sister to Saint Kevin and the mother of seven saints.

MEALLÁN m. (mall-awn) From "lightning." There were three recorded saints of this name.

NIAMH f. (nee-av) "brightness, luster, radiance." An early divine name that occurs frequently in mythology. The fairy woman Niamh Chinn Óir ("of the golden head") seduced Oisín, son of Finn, and took him off to the Land of Promise or Tir na n'Óg, where, unwittingly he spent 300 years in what he thought were three weeks. Currently popular in Ireland, Néamh is another less-used Irish form. Neve is a recent form found in the United States.

ORLA/Órlaith f. "golden princess." The fourth most popular female name in twelfth-century Ireland, it was shared by both a sister and a niece of Brian Boru. It seems to have fallen from favor for a long time thereafter but has become very popular in recent times. Orlagh is another form.

SORCHA f. (sur-'cha) "bright, radiant." A name widely used in the Middle Ages and up to the nineteenth century. In the past, it was Anglicized as Sally and Sarah. Currently finding renewed popularity in Britain and Ireland.

A Celtic Menagerie

§ A large class of early Irish names derive from the names of animals. Certain animals, notably the bear and the wolf, were taboo, and could not be directly invoked in language. Instead, descriptive terms such as *fáelán,* ''the howler,'' or *mac tíre,* ''son of the land,'' were used to refer to these creatures. In time, these terms were used for first names, which could impart some of the power of these animals to the bearer. The word for a wolf or a hound, *cu* or *con,* is a well-favored element in many early names. The hound was appreciated as loyal and valorous in conflict, ideal qualities befitting a warrior. Some early animal terms are associated with particular divinities and take their name from these sources; Fainche is a word for a crow but is also the name of an early war goddess.

The following is a selection of names recorded that are connected with animal names or qualities. Of course, contemporary tastes may demur at some inclusions; Banbhan (banvan) may be all very well when it comes to contemporary phonetic tastes, but its associations, a suckling pig, are a little raw for today's mores. The animal lover will, however, find much to delight in here, and while it may be too much to hope for a next generation of Cúmhaís and Ailchús, there is no harm in wishing to greet a future wave of Brocks and Cuans, Ronaits and Earcs.

AILCHÚ m. (al-chu) "gentle hound."

ART m. "a bear." This old name has had a long pedigree in Ireland. As a word for bear, it was only ever used as a personal name or in a figurative appraisal of someone, as the bear was a taboo animal who could not directly be invoked. Kings and warriors have shared the name, and it remains in use today. Artán, Artagán, and Airtín are pet forms. It has traditionally been Anglicized as Arthur, with which it has no real connection.

BANBHÁN m. (ban-van) "a piglet, a sucking pig." An early name recorded as that belonging to two saints.

BANBHNAIT f. (banv-nit) The feminine form of Banbhán, also recorded as the name for two female saints.

BÓINN f. (boyn) "cow-white." The name of an early goddess associated with the Boyne River, mother of the love god Aengus.

BRADEN m. A form of the surname used as a first name, especially in the United States. From the Irish *bradán,* "salmon." Bradon and Brayden are other forms.

BRAN m. "a raven." One of the most popular early Celtic names, used throughout Europe as far east as Greece. The name occurs repeatedly in legend as that of a god, champions, poets, and saints. Recently, it has been used as a name for dogs, as legend has it that Finn Mac Cool's wolfhound bore the name. Brannan is a pet form, as is the surname Brannigan.

BRANCHÚ m. (bran-chu) A composite name of *bran,* "raven," and *cu,* "hound."

BROC/Brock m. (bruk) "a badger." A relatively uncommon early name from which probably derives the surname Brock, which has also more recently been used as a first name. Brocán is a pet form.

BROICSEACH f. (brik-shok) a feminine diminutive of Broc.

BROTCHÚ m. (brut-chu) Perhaps "thieving hound."

CADHAN m. (kein) "a wild goose, a barnacle goose." A very early name, from which we get the surname O Cadhain. Anglicized as Kyne.

CANA m. (kon-a) "a wolf cub," or a title meaning a young warrior. Cannanan and Cannagan are diminutive forms.

CIONNAOLA m. (kin-aola) From Cenn Faelad, "wolf head." A very popular early name. One distinguished bearer was Cenn Faelad, son of Ailill, who was the earliest known record maker of Irish law. The surname O Cionnaola comes from this name, and has been Anglicized as Kennelly.

COILEÁN m. (kil-awn) "a whelp," and by extension, "a youth, a young warrior." A common early name in the south.

COLM m. (colum) A name deriving from the Latin *columba*, "a dove." As a symbol of peace, the name became a popular choice for the Christianized Irish wishing to revoke earlier warlike ways. There are some thirty-two recorded saints who bore the name, the most famous of which is Columba of Iona, known as Colmcille, "Colm of the church," who founded an influential monastery on Iona. Colum and Columb are other forms, with Callum or Calum being the favored Scottish forms.

COLMA f. feminine form of Colman.

COLMAN m. A diminutive of Colm, hence "little dove." Colman became a very popular name in early Ireland, and texts record no less than 234 saints who bore the name. The most famous, perhaps, was the sixth-century bishop known as Columbanus and Columban, who founded monasteries throughout Europe, becoming a popular devotional figure in France, Italy, Slovakia, the Czech Republic, and Hungary, where the name became variously Colombain, Columbano, Kolman, and Kalman. Colman and Columb were also used in the past as girls' names, though they rarely occur today. Cóilín is a pet form popular in the west.

CONALL m. (kun-al) "strong as a wolf." A popular early name borne by kings and warriors of note. Conall Corc ("the red") was a fifth-century king of Munster who founded the influential kingship of Cashel. Connell is the Anglicized form.

CONÁN m. (kun-awn) "hound, wolf." An old name with recent associations in the figures of author Arthur Conan Doyle, who created Sherlock Holmes, and in the fictional character of Robert B. Howard's Conan the Barbarian, both of whom use the Anglophone pronunciation. Conant is another form.

CONGHAL m. (kun-yl) "brave as a wolf." Another popular early name borne by kings in the past With the similar but distinctive Conall, it has been Anglicized, Connell. Conghalach (kun-ilach) is a pet form.

CONMHAC m. (kun-vok) "wolf son, hound son." Anglicized Canoc.

CONN/Con m. This name may be interpreted as meaning "sense, intelligence," and was thence used to mean "chief, head," but it has associations with the name element *cu*, meaning "hound, wolf." The legendary figure of Conn Cead Cathach ("of the hundred battles") is the most famous bearer of the name. The province of Connacht was named for him, and the O'Neills, O'Donnells, O'Connors, O'Flahertys, and O'Dowds are among those claiming him as an ancestor. In Donegal, the name has long been of particular importance. It was Anglicized as Constantine, which still occurs in Ireland today.

CONOR/Connor m. This is the Anglicized form of the old name Conchobhar (kru-hoor), meaning "wolf lover, lover of hounds." It has remained popular in Ireland for centuries. Conchobhar Mac Nessa is a legendary king of Ulster who was popularly elected as ruler, but later is characterized as ruthless in his treatment of Deirdre and her lover Naoise. The name has been shortened and altered in various forms throughout its usage, occurring as the Latin, unrelated Cornelius, as Nelius, Corney, Curney, Neil, Neelusheen, Cony, Con, Cud, Nahor, Naugher, Nohor, and in Ireland more recently as Conchur. Connor is the most popular spelling of the name in the United States today, where it is also rendered Conner. In 1997, as Conor, it ranked fifth in the top ten names chosen for boys in Ireland.

CONRÍ m. (con-ree) Composed of separate name elements *con,* "wolf, hound" and *ri,* "king." An early name perhaps best Anglicized as Conry.

CRIOFAN/Criomhthann m. (kree-fan) "a fox." One of the most popular names in early Ireland, shared by kings, warriors, and saints, it is rarely encountered today. Perhaps the unwieldy spelling is partly to blame. Shortened Anglicized forms seem to have strayed far from the source. Creon, Crehan, Crevan, Criffin, and Griffin are some of the various ways it has been rendered.

CUACH f. (koo-ach) Literally, "cuckoo." Contemporary associations with this name are probably unkind.

CUAN m. (koo-an) Similar to the name Conan, this name is a pet form of *cu,* "hound, wolf." *Cu* was a common element in warrior names and represented bravery and loyalty. Cúchulainn is the most famous Irish legendary warrior and took his name to mean "hound of Culann," the man who he chose to serve after he had slain Culann's guard dog in self-defense. Cuan is a name of growing popularity in Ireland today.

CÚMHAÍ/Cú Mhaighe m. (koo-vee) A name with some popularity in the Middle Ages, it means "hound of the plain." It has been Anglicized as Quintin or Quinton, names with which it has no real connection.

DARERCA/Darearca f. (dar-ark-a) "daughter of Erc," *erc* being a name for a salmon. This name has been shared by four female saints, one of whom in legend was said to be the mother of seventeen bishops and sister to Saint Patrick.

DAVIN/Damhán/Daimhín m. This is the Anglicized form of the older Irish names Daimhín, "ox, deer," and Damhán its diminutive, "little ox, little stag." Davan is another Anglicized form.

DAVNIT/Damhnait f. "fawn, little deer." A name that has occured in various forms in history and legend. Most famously, it is associated with two saints, one of whom is associated with Slieve Beagh and Tedavnet, County Monaghan, and whose crosier is preserved in the National Museum, Dublin. The other, who is more widely known as Saint Dymphna, was martyred in Belgium and is venerated as the patron saint of the insane. Devnit, Downet, Dymphna, and Dympna are other Anglicized forms.

DONNCUAN m. (dun-koo-an) "Donn of the hound pack." Donn is a name that could mean "dun, brown" or "king, lord." Donncuan is an early name and one of its distinguished bearers was the brother of Ireland's famous high king, Brian Boru.

EACHA m. (ach-a) "horselike" or "horse god." In Irish mythology Eacha is husband to the goddess Áine.

EACHIARN/Eachthiaghearn m. (ach-iarn) "lord of steeds." A relatively common early name, from which derives the contemporary surname Aherne.

EACHNA f. (ach-na) From the word element *ech*, "a steed." Eachna in legend was daughter to the king of Connacht and she was said to be the cleverest and most beautiful woman of her time.

EACRHA f. (ach-ra) Another feminine name from the term for a horse, *ech*. Eachra was a tenth-century princess, renowned for her beautiful complexion.

ÉANNA m. (aon-a) Traditionally, this name is interpreted to mean "birdlike." It was a name borne by a number of early kings, one of whom, in the sixth century, converted to Christianity and founded several monasteries before settling on Inishmore in the Aran Islands, with which, as Saint Éanna, he has become associated. Enda is the popular Anglicized form.

EARC/Erc f. & m. (ark) A word meaning either "speckled, dark red" or "a salmon." A fairly common early name used for both men and women. In legend, Earc was a resourceful woman who revived her slain lover by placing in his mouth an herb she had seen a weasel use to revive her dead mate.

EILTÍN m. (el-teen) Derived from *elit,* meaning "a hind," which is a young deer, or otherwise, "a lively, nimble person." It might be Anglicized Eltin.

EINÍN f. (a-neen) A contemporary name meaning "little bird."

EOCHAIDH/Eochaí m. (yo-ee) "horse rider." This, along with its pet form Eochu, was the second most popular name in early Irish society. Kings, poets, and saints have borne the name. Eochaidh Airem was the legendary lover of Etain.

Various Anglicized and pet forms have evolved including Oghie, Oghe, Oho, Ataigh, Atty, and Eoi.

FÁILBHE m. (fall-ve) An old name meaning "wolf slayer," or perhaps "a lively, spritely person."

FAINCHE f. (fine-she) Meaning "a scald-crow." Originally probably a name used for the Irish goddess of war, later the name was borne by some fourteen saints. Saint Fainche of Rossory at Lough Erne was sister to Saint Éanna of Arran and an important influence in his life. The name has been rendered as Fanchea and Faenche and Anglicized as Fanny.

FAOLÁN m. (fway-lawn) "wolf." A common early name found in royal, religious, and secular life. Some fourteen saints bore the name, as well as three kings of Leinster. The name has been Anglicized as Felan and Phelan and gives the surnames O'Phelan, O'Whelan, and Hyland.

FAOLCHÚ m. (fwayl-'hu) "wolf, wolfhound."

FEENAT/Fiadhnait/Fianait f. (fee-'nit) "wild creature, deer." A name shared by two saints in the past. Also found in Anglicized form as Feena.

FEICHÍN m. (feh-een) A name that may come from the words for "raven" or "battle." Five Irish saints bore the name, the most famous of which was Feichín of Fore, in Scotland, where he was also known as Vigean. An Irish pet name for Saint Feichín was Mo-Ecca, and the name has been rendered as Festus, Festie, and Fehin.

FIACH m. (fee-ach) The source for this name is the Irish word *fiach*, "raven," though it may be a pet form of Fiacre. Fiacha is another form.

FIACRE/Fiachra m. (fee-acra) This name probably derives from the old Irish word for "raven," *fiach*, but some have interpreted it to mean "battle king." It was a popular early name with records of use by both saints and kings. Saint Fiacre of Meaux was an Irish hermit who settled in France, where his name eventually came to be used for the Parisian taxicabs operating in and around the Hotel Saint-Fiacre. Inevitably, he has come to be seen as a patron saint of travelers. Peculiarly enough, his patronage extends further to embrace both horticultural workers and sufferers of sexually transmitted diseases. Fiacre is still a popular name in Ireland to date. Feary is an Anglicized form.

FIAMAIN f. (fiev-in) "swift-footed creature."

GEILÉIS/Gelgéis f. (gel-ace) "bright swan." A name recorded as used by an early princess. Gelace could be an Anglicized form.

LAOGH m. (lay-ugh) "calf."

LONÁN m. Derived from the word *lon*, "blackbird." Some eleven saints are said to have borne the name.

MAHON/Mathúin m. A shortened form of Mathghamhain, "bear calf," (bear cub) which was the name of a tenth-century king of Cashel, brother of Brian Boru. Mahon, the Anglicized form is more usually found as a contemporary surname in Ireland. Surnames O'Mahoney and MacMahon also originate from this name.

MARCÁN m. (mark-awn) A name derived from the Irish *marc,* "a steed."

MOCHULLA m. (mu-chol-a) A pet form for Colm with recorded use by thirteen saints.

MUGHRÓN m. (mu-rone) A popular early name meaning, perhaps, "lad of the seals."

MURPHY f. & m. This popular Irish surname derives from the Irish *murchú,* "hound of the sea." It has found increasing favor as a first name for both boys and girls in the United States.

NESSÁN/Neasan m. One possible meaning for this name is "stoat." It was borne by some five saints of record.

ODHAR m. (or) This name is usually interpreted to mean "dark, sallow, gray-brown," but is also possibly the old Irish term for an otter, here used as a personal name.

OISÍN m. (ush-een) "little deer." In legend, Oisín was the son of Finn Mac Cool, who left Ireland with Niamh for the fairy land, Tir na n'Óg, "land of the young." What seemed like a short stay to Oisín translated into 300 years upon his return, and once his foot touched the soil, he instantly aged to an old, old man. Ossian is an Anglicized form, but the name has popularly retained its Irish spelling in Ireland, where it has enjoyed a fashionable resurgence in the last twenty years.

ONCHÚ m. (un-khu) "fierce hound."

ORNA/Odharnait/Órnait f. Feminine form of Odhar, "an otter."

OSCAR m. "deer lover." In legend, Oscar was the grandson of Finn Mac Cool and son of Oisín. In time, he became leader of the Fianna, the royal bodyguard, and was the most celebrated warrior of his day. His deeds were celebrated by the Scottish poet James Macpherson, whose work became very popular throughout Europe, eventually coming to the attention of Napoleon Bonaparte. Bonaparte bequeathed the name to a godson, who eventually became part of the royal lineage of Sweden. It has since enjoyed great popularity in Scandinavia. The name fell from favor in Britain and Ireland after the trials and scandal surrounding its most famous bearer, Oscar Wilde. It is currently regaining some of its popularity there and has always been in use in the United States.

OSSÁN m. (us-awn) "little deer."

OSSNAT/Osnait f. (os-nit) Feminine form of Ossan.

RONAIT/Ronnad f. (ron-it) A feminine form of Ronan.

RONAN m. From *rón*, "a seal." This was a popular early name and has been recorded as used by some ten saints. Saint Ronan Finn (d. 664) placed a curse on his tormentor, Suibhne Gelt, who subsequently went mad and spent the rest of his life wandering the country as the mad birdman of legend.

SEANAIT f. (sha-nit) From the Irish *seig*, "a hawk." Shaylee and Shaylyn are contemporary elaborations from this name.

SHAY/Shea m. From the Irish *Seaghdha,* "hawklike, fine." The surname O'Shea derives from this name.

TORCÁN m. (turk-awn) A name derived from the word *torcc,* "a wild boar."

The Green Isle

§ The natural vegetation of the country was well observed by the early Irish and celebrated in name forms. Early arrivals to the country would have found a land thickly forested with a variety of deciduous trees, and names recording the various species were commonly deployed, initially as first names, then later as surnames with the prefix Mac-. Because of the land's dense forrestation, which took centuries to clear, the central plain of Meath, with its level surface and clear horizon, became a central focus of settlement and defense, giving rise to the celebrated royal site of Tara. The following list is a selection of names, some early, some more recent in pedigree, that draw their inspiration from the flora of Ireland.

ABHLACH f. (av-loch) "having apple trees." The name of a ninth-century princess.

ANBHILE m. (an-vile) "great tree."

BLÁITHÍN f. (blaw-heen) "flowerlet, little blossom." A name with a long history of use in Ireland, translated from time to time as Florence.

BLÁTH f. (blaw) "flower, blossom."

BLÁTHNAIT/Blánaid/Bláthnat/Bláthnaid f. (blaw-nid) Another form of Bláithín, a diminutive of Bláth, "little flower." In legend, Bláthnait was the reluctant wife of Cú Roí. She fell in love with Cúchulainn, her husband's rival, and revealed to him the secret entrance to her husband's fortress by pouring milk into an outflowing stream. Cúchulainn vanquished the fortress and took Bláthnait as his prize. Cú Roí's poet, in an act of desperate vengeance, grabbed Bláthnait and jumped with her to their deaths from the clifftop of Cenn Bera.

CARMEL f. A popular imported Catholic name in Ireland, used in reverence to Our Lady of Mount Carmel. From the Hebraic word for "garden."

CRAOBHNAIT f. (crev-nit) From *croeb*, "a branch, a garland."

CROEB f. (crev) "a branch, a garland."

DÁIRE m. (daw-re) "fruitful, to make fertile." This is a name occurring frequently in early Irish legend, probably the name for a divinity, a bull god. In earliest times, it was used by both women and men, but later became used exclusively for boys. The name might be Anglicized as Darragh, and Derry has been used as a pet form.

DÁITHÍ m. (daw-hee) A form of the older name Nathí or Naithí, "nephew of Eo," hence "nephew of a tree." In the Middle Ages, the name was equated with the word *daithe,* "swiftness," and became Dáithí. Dathy is another form, and Dahy the Anglicization. In the past, it has been used as a form for Dáibhí, the Irish way of writing Davy.

DARA/Darragh f. & m. A shortened form of the name Mac Dara, "son of the oak." The name was used formerly only for men but in later years has found some popularity as a girl's name.

DARINA/Dáirine f. (da-reen-na) Probably a feminine form of the name Dáire. Darina was a princess, daughter of the High King Tuathal Teachtmar, unknowingly involved in a bigamous wedding to Eochaidh, king of Leinster. When it was discovered that Eochaidh's supposed late wife, Darina's elder sister Fithir, was still alive, both she and her sister died of shame. Their father went to war with Leinster and extracted tribute for generations thereafter.

DARREN m. A name derived probably from Dara or Darragh. In the twentieth century, it took hold in America as early as the twenties and had a surge of popularity in the sixties and seventies, posssibly in connection with the successful television series *Bewitched.* There are many contemporary variant forms including Daren, Darin, Darran, Darrin, Darron, and Derron.

DRAIGHEAN f. (drain) An early Irish name possibly connected with the word *draigen,* meaning "blackthorn."

EASCRACH f. (as-krach) "blooming, blossoming." An early saint's name.

EITHNE f. (eth-na) A name with an ancient pedigree in Ireland, probably originally the name of a divinity. From *eithne,* "kernel," and "of a nut," or possibly from *aitten,* "gorse." This was the third most popular female name in early Ireland. One Eithne was the mother of the sun god Lugh. Another, Eithne of the Tuatha Dé Danann—the original fairy people of Ireland—lost her demon guardian and crossed over to become a Christian. Many queens and some nine saints have borne the name. Other forms are Ethna, Etna, and Enya, and it has been Anglicized an Edna and Ena.

EOGHAN/Eógan m. (owen) "born of the yew." This was a very popular early name, giving rise to a variety of family strains, among them the Eoghanacht, "race of Eoghan," and the Cenel Eógan, descendants of Niall of the Nine Hostages. It has been Anglicized as Owen, the Welsh form of Eugene, "well-born," which is an unconnected name, and thence as Oyne and Oynie. In Scotland, it takes the form of Ewan, Ewen, Euan, and Evan. It is easily confused with the name Eoin, pronouced similarly, which is an Irish form of the biblical name John. Eoghanán (own-awn) is a pet form.

FINA/Fíona f. (fee-na) Fina is the Anglicized form of the old Irish name Fíne, written as Fíona in modern Irish. It derives from the latin *vinea,* "vine." The Anglo-Scots name, Fiona, popularly used in Ireland today, is of a separate origin.

FINSCOTH f. (fin-sku) "wine blossom." In legend, Finscoth was the daughter of Cuchulainn.

FRAOCH m. (fray-och) From *fraech,* "heather." Fraoch Mac Fidaig of Connacht, son of the fairy woman Bé Finn, appears in saga as the most handsome man in all of Ireland and Scotland. Fraochán (fray-ochawn) is a diminutive.

IOBHAR/Ivar m. (ee-var) "yew." A popular early name, recorded as that of an inspirational saint on Beggerin Island, who was vehemently opposed to the mission of another inspirational figure, Saint Patrick himself.

JACINTA f. A Spanish name that has found some popularity in recent times in Ireland. From hyacinth.

LABHRÁS m. (law-raws) "a laurel bush."

MAC CÁIRTHINN m. (mac-corhin) "son of the rowan tree." A saint's name, which has been Anglicized as Macartan.

MAC COILLE m. (mac-kila) "son of the wood." In ecclesiastical legend, Saint Mac Coille was Saint Patrick's nephew.

MAC CUILINN m. (mac-kilin) "son of the holly."

MAC DARA m. "son of the oak." Saint Mac Dara of Connemara is a patron of local fishermen.

NONÍN f. (no-neen) A name of fairly recent pedigree. From *nonín,* the Irish for "daisy."

ROISIN/Róisín f. (ro-sheen) This is the more popular pet form of the name Róis, derived from the English name Rose. Language experts insist that the origins of this name are unconnected with the flower but stem from the old German word *hros,* meaning "horse." It is unlikely that the name owes its continued popularity to this source and, imaginatively, it is now attached to the flower of the same name, from the Latin *rosa.* Records begin to reveal its use in

Ireland in the sixteenth century. In the figure of Róisín Dubh, from the song of the same title, the name became associated with a poetic personification of Ireland and her nationalist yearnings. This song title is translated to English as "Dark Rosaleen," and both forms of the name have enjoyed popularity in Ireland. Rosheen, Rosalie, and Rosaline are other forms.

SCOITHÍN m. (sku-heen) From *scoth*, "bloom, blossom."

SCOITHNIAMH f. (sku-niav) Compound of *scoth*, "a bloom, a blossom," and *niam*, "shining, lustrous." An attractive name that begs for a contemporary Anglicized spelling.

SCOTH f. (skuh) "bloom, blossom."

SCOTHNAIT f. (sku-nit) A feminine form of Scoithín.

SÚSANNA f. (soo-sana) This is the Irish form of the old Hebraic name Susannah, meaning "lily." The pet forms Susie and Sue were rendered Sósaidh (so-see) and Siúi (su-ee).

TYRONE m. From the Irish county of the same name, Tir Eoghan, "land of Eoghan." Popularized in the twentieth century by figures such as famed theater director, Tyrone Guthrie, and film actor, Tyrone Power, themselves related through a Waterford-born great-grandfather. U.S. forms of this name are Tyron and Ty, and recent feminine elaborations Taryn, Tarin, Teryn, and Tyra.

UAINE f. (uan-e) "green, verdant." In the Finn legends, Uaine appears as an enchanting musician.

UAITHNE f. & m. (u-enya) "greenish." A name with a long history of usage, which eventually gave rise to a tribal name. Anglicized as Oney, Owney, Oynie, Hewney, and—through translation—Greene.

The Fighting Irish

Celtic society was a complex tribal structure with many conventions of heirarchy and allegiance. The smallest tribe grouping was known as a *tuatha,* and by around the sixth century, there numbered about 150 of these throughout the country. Each tuatha had its own ruler, who was in turn subordinate to an overking who might rule three or more such groups. In turn, this king would be subject to a higher king, usually the claimant of a province from one of several dominant family lines. The overkings maintained uneasy strategic alliances with each other. As one might expect, there was rarely an occasion when all was at peace with such a structure. Warfare between tuatha, petty kingdoms, and provincial rulers was endemic. This situation continued well up until the end of the Middle Ages, when whatever long-term differences stood between land-owning families were crushed beneath the greater perceived threat of Anglo domination. Given this situation, it is not surprising to learn that warlike names occur from the earliest records and that the later adoption of imported Norman names still reflects a taste for the battle-hardened and contentious. Some of these names are very familiar to us today, though their original interpretations may have faded into obscurity and have been replaced by more contemporary associations.

ÁGHMACH m. (awch) A name from legend, "contentious, warlike."

AICHEAR m. (e-har) "sharp, keen, fierce." In the Finn tales, Aichear appears as one of the musicians of the Fianna. From this name derives the modern surname O'Hehir and probably O'Hare. A contemporary Anglicization might be Ehir.

ALOYSIUS m. (alu-wish-as) This is an imported name, a Latinized form of Louis, meaning "famous warrior." In Ireland, the name was popularly used in reverence of Saint Aloysius Gonzaga, a Jesuit of the sixteenth century. Alaois (al-aysh) and Alabhaois (ala-waysh) are Irish forms.

BEARACH m. (bar-ach or bar-a) "pointed, sharp." This was a well-used name in early Ireland and is one source for the contemporary name Barry. Several saints of record have borne the name, one of whom, from the sixth century, was credited with miracle-working, including raising the dead.

BERCAN/Bearchán m. (bar-chawn or bar-awn) A diminutive of Bearach. Some seven saints are known to have borne the name. Barhan is another appropriate Anglicized form.

BRASSAL/Breasal m. (bra-sil) "brave or strong in conflict." A popular early name with regal association. Well-used through to the later Middle Ages, it has assumed a variety of forms, including Brasil, Brassal, Brazil, Bresal, and Brissal, with diminutives Breaslan, Breslan, and Breslin.

BRENDA f. This name is really from the old Norse *brandr,* likely meaning the blade of a sword, but is popularly construed as a feminine form of the Irish name Brendan. Walter Scott is credited with popularizing it when he used it in his novel of 1821, *The Pirate.* Widely used since then, it reached a peak of popularity in the 1940s.

BUACH/Buagh/Buadhach m. (boo-ach) "victorious." A name associated with the south and especially the O'Sullivans. Buachan occurs as a diminutive and Buanait as a feminine form. The first-century warrior queen of Britain, Boadicea, takes her name from a common Celtic root.

CAHIR/Cathaoir m. (care) Popularly interpreted to mean "battle lord." Cathaoir Mór is a legendary Leinster high king reputed to have reigned for fifty years and to have fathered thirty-three sons. Cahir is an early Anglicized form used by Cahir O'Doherty, who rose to prominence during the reign of Elizabeth I. In the past Cahir was translated as Charles, an unconnected name.

CASEY f. & m. This name derives from the common early Irish name Cathasach, "vigilant in war." It has been quietly used as a first name for some time in Ireland and the United States, but in the twentieth century was made famous in the figure of Jonathan Luther "Casey" Jones (1864–1900), the engine driver on the Cannon Ball Express, who saved the lives of many of his passengers by sacrificing his own. Presently proving very popular in the United States as a girl's name, it has taken on many various forms including Casie, Kacie, Kaci, Kacee, Kacey, and Kasey.

CATHACH f. (ka-hach) "warlike." In legend, Cathach was a warrior woman who loved the Ulster hero Cúchulainn.

CATHAL/Cahal m. (ka-hal) From the elements *cath*, "battle," and *val*, "rule," hence the interpretation "strong in battle." A very common name in the early Middle Ages, Cathal has regained some of its popularity in the twentieth century, probably in association with the figure of Cathal Brugha (1874–1922), a Republican soldier and politician during the civil war. The standard translation has regularly been Charles, a name with which it has no connection.

CEARBHALL/Cearúl m. (kar-ool) "brave in fighting, valorous in battle." A name with a record of royal usage and popular in the Middle Ages with Leinster aristocracy. Later, a name favored by the O'Daly (O Dáilaigh) family. Cearbhall O Dáilaigh (1911–1978) was the fifth president of the Irish Republic. Also used frequently in its less daunting, Anglicized form, Carroll.

CONNERY/Conaire m. "warrior lord." More usually encountered as a surname, Connery has a history of usage by the O'Clery family. In legend Conaire Mór ("the great"), also known as Conaire Caomh ("the gentle"), was a high king of Tara renowned for his wise rule.

ÉIGNEACH m. (ayg-nach) Probably from the word *ecen*, "force." Éigneachán (ayg-nach-awn) is a diminutive that was popularly used in the fifteenth and sixteenth centuries, especially among the O'Donnells, O'Dohertys, and O'Kellys.

FERGAL/Fearghal m. (fer-gal or fer-il). This name is interpreted as meaning "valorous" or "manly." Very common in early Ireland, it is still prevalent today. Fergal Mac Maoldúin was an eighth-century high king renowned for his deeds in battle. From the same century, we get Saint Fergal, known also as Saint Vergil, who became bishop of Salzburg. The surnames O'Farrell and Farrell derive from this name.

FIACHRA/Fiacre m. (fee-acra) One interpretation of this well-used early name is "battle king," the other being "raven." In mythology, Fiachra was one of the bewitched children of the sea god Lir, who was transformed into a swan by his jealous stepmother, Aoife. Fiacha occurs sometimes as a pet form.

GARRETT/Garret/Gearóid m. (garret or gar-ode) One of the names arising from the popular Germanic names Gerald, "spear rule," and Gerard, "spear brave," introduced to Ireland by the Normans. Gearóid is the Gaelic form and is widely used to translate both Gerald and Gerard, but the more Anglophonic Garret has proved popular this century.

GARVIN/Garvan/Garbhán m. From *garb,* "rough." Five saints of record are known to have borne the name.

GERALD/Gearalt/Gearóid m. From the Germanic "spear rule." This name came to Ireland from the Normans, particularly with the FitzGeralds, who established an 800-year-long dynasty that tied Ireland to Britain. In Irish, it was rendered Gearalt and Gearóid, and all forms of the name have been used regularly, including the later form, Garrett.

GERALDINE f. The name may be interpreted as a feminine form of Gerald, but in truth it originates from the personage of Lady Elizabeth FitzGerald, of the titled Kildare family. The sixteenth-century courtier-poet Surrey alluded to the lady as "the Fair Geraldine," and it was then that the name was born. In the nineteenth century, the name began to be widely used in all English-speaking countries, possibly popularized by Coleridge in his poem "Christabel," and has remained very popular in Ireland. The name is rendered Gearóidín (gar-o-deen) in Irish. Ger is a commonly used shortened form.

GERARD/Gearárd m. Germanic, "spear brave." Another name introduced by the Normans, along with the similar sounding Gerald. In the past, Gerard was rather overwhelmed by Gerald, but has since become the preferred choice, possibly due to the popularity of the eighteenth-century figure of Saint Gerard Majella, the patron saint of motherhood and childbirth. Very prevalent in Ireland today where it is frequently shortened to Gerry, Jerry, or Ger. Gearóid is the most commonly used Irish form today.

KANE/Cathán m. From *cath*, "battle," hence, "battler." A name from the west, which took hold in the north giving the surname Ó Catháin (O'Kane), a prominent Ulster family. Used infrequently in the past, the Anglicized form, Kane, began to be more popularly used in the sixties, especially in Australia and then in the United States. Kaine and Kayne are other forms. Cathán, abbess of Kildare in the ninth century, reveals an early female use of the name.

KILLIAN/Cillian m. (kil-ian) One possible meaning of this name derives from *cill*, "a church." Another source is thought to be a word meaning "strife." Nevertheless, the name has long been connected with several saints of record. One, Saint Killian of Würzburg, is a martyr venerated in Germany. The name, also spelled Kilian, is still common in Ireland.

LONEGAN/Lonergan/Lonargán m. From the words *lonn,* "bold, eager," and *garg,* "rough, fierce." Chiefly today encountered as a surname.

LORCAN/Lorcán m. From *lorc,* "cruel" or "fierce." This was a popular name in the early Middle Ages, with a history of royal usage. One Lorcan was an ancestor of Brian Boru. Two kings of Leinster bore the name. Saint Lorcan O Tuathail, better known as Saint Laurence O'Toole, was an influential bishop of Dublin in the twelfth century. Laurence, the traditional translation used, is really an unconnected name.

MACHA f. (moch-a) An old name that occurs in legend as that of a war goddess. Navan fort, or Emain Macha, was named for another Macha, as was the site of the town of Armagh, which comes from Ard Macha, "the height of Macha." There is a saint of record, a patroness of Killiney, County Kerry, who also bore the name.

MÁIRTÍN m. (mar-cheen) This is the Irish form of Martin, which comes from the Latin name meaning "belonging to Mars." Mars was the preeminent Latin god of war. Its use in Ireland, however, was with reference to the saintly figure of Saint Martin of Tours, who was himself a soldier during the fourth century. Martán is another, earlier Irish form.

MAOLÁN/Máelán m. (mayl-awn) "a warrior." An early name, today it occurs in the contemporary surname O Maoláin, or as O'Mullan or Mullins.

NIALL m. (neel) This is the most commonly used Irish form of the name more popularly Anglicized as Neil or Neal. It has had a long history of usage in Ireland and occurs in various forms, including those mentioned above, as well as

Neill, Néill, Neale, Nial, and Niel. In some instances, the pronunciation becomes "nye-al." Its meaning is debated, some thinking it to mean "passionate, vehement," some thinking it to derive from a word for "champion." Another theory is that it is connected with the word *nel*, meaning cloud. Nevertheless, all agree that its continued use was with regard to its most famous bearer, Niall Naoi-ghiallach (nee-eealach) or Niall of the Nine Hostages, a fifth-century king and ancestor of the O'Nialls, whose deeds have passed into legend. The name Nigel originates from a Latin rendering of Niall, and the name Nelson derives from the related surname.

SCÁTHACH f. (skaw-hoch) "shadowy, ghostly, frightening." In legend, Scáthach was a fairy woman who taught the young hero Cúchulainn the use of weapons.

TREASACH m. (tras-ach) "warlike, fierce." An early name that gave rise to the surnames O'Tracey and Treacy.

UINSEANN m. (in-shen) The Irish form of the Latin-originating name Vincent, "conquering." Used with reference to the sixteenth-century figure, Saint Vincent de Paul.

Wednesday's Child

Evidence suggests that our Irish ancestors were quite taken with the notion of naming their offspring for certain sorrowful episodes, or after qualities that could not, even back then, have been viewed as wholly admirable. Names like Duarcan ("sad, melancholy"), Fann ("a tear"), Fionghuine ("kin slayer") and Baoth ("vain, reckless"), all proved popular over lengthy periods of time. It is conceivable that some of these names may have been given later in a person's life, after they had distinguished themselves by certain traits of behavior or certain misdeeds. Eigeartach ("wrongdoer") and Fogarta ("outlaw") are names suggesting a particular action on the part of the bearer. Typically, the names may have been passed down in family usage as a form of homage to an earlier ancestor.

Then again, it is possible that usually these names were used without consideration of their original meanings or connotations, just the way someone today might use the name James without any thought of the original Hebrew meaning of "he who takes by the heel, a supplanter," or the name

Mary without regard for a possible interpretation meaning "bitterness."

The picture of a society that was willing to embrace the less worthy traits of human nature, to solemnize painful incidents in individual experience by naming a child for them, is an attractive one contrasted with these times of insistent, noisy celebration. The following is a gallery of such names, some of them perhaps familiar, some perhaps best left in the past, and a few—one finally hopes—ready for revival.

AINBHEARTACH m. (an-vart-och) "doer of evil deeds." Ahem. Old southern name.

AINFEACH m. (an-fawch) "stormy, tempestuous."

AINFEAN f. (an-fan) "storm, fury." A name borne, peculiarly enough, by a virgin saint.

AINMIRE m. (an-vir-e) Meaning perhaps "wicked lord" as well as "great lord." Borne by an early high king and recorded as the name of two saints. Anglicized as Anvirre.

AINNÍLEAS m. (an-eel-as) "child of uncertain parentage."

ANFUDÁN m. (an-fawn) "turbulent, tempestuous, fiery person."

ÁRCHÚ m. (ar-choo) "hound of slaughter."

BAOTH m. (bay) "vain, reckless, wanton, foolish." A relatively common early name with well-used diminutives: Baothán (bay-awn), Baolach (bay-loch), and Baoithín/Beheen (bi-heen).

BEIRGÍN m. (ber-geen) "a brigand, a robber, a soldier." Anglicized as Bergin.

BÉTÉIDE f. (be-tay-de) A legendary figure, Bétéide was one of the fairy folk the Tuatha Dé Danann. Her name means literally "wanton woman."

BREAS m. (br-as) A mythological name that could mean "fight, uproar, din," as well as "shapely, beautiful."

BRENNAN/Braonán/Braon/Bren m. From Braon, probably meaning "drop of water," hence "a tear." In Ireland, mostly a surname, but currently being used in the United States as a first name with various spellings: Brenen, Brennen, Brennon, Brennyn, and Branon.

BRONA/Brónach/Bronagh/Brone f. "sorrowful." A saint's name, rarely used in early times, it has become quite popular in Ireland more recently.

CACHT f. & m. (kocht) "slave, bondmaid."

COMYN/Cuimín/Coman m. (co-min) "crooked."

CORB/Corbb m. (kurb) From the verb *corbbaid,* "defile." A name used in early legend only, with recorded usage of diminutives Corbban and Corbbéne. Corban is an Anglicized form of the diminutive.

CORMAC/Cormacc m. Probably from compound of Corb and *mac,* "son of Corb." A name with a long history of usage from early times up to the present. Kings, saints, and warriors have borne this name, including early patrons of the O'Niall, O'Brien, and MacNamara families. Cormac Mac Art

is one of the great legendary high kings of Ireland, the father
of Grania and regent to Finn Mac Cool. Cormaccán is a
diminutive.

DALLAN/Dallán m. (dol-awn) "blind one." A widely used
older name associated with early poets of note, and specifically used around Kildallan, County Cavan, which takes its
name from a saint of the same name.

DOIREANN/Dorean/Doirind f. (der-ann or dor-ean) Traditionally interpreted to mean "sullen," the name has since
been linked with Dairinn, "daughter of Finn." Doirind was
one of the daughters of Midhir Yellow-mane in Irish legend.
The more popular name Doreen is thought to be an Irish
derivation of this old form.

DOLORES f. From the Spanish title for the Virgin Mary,
Maria de los Dolores, "Mary of the sorrows." Popularly
used as a Catholic first name in Ireland today.

DORAN/Dorran m. From the Irish surname O Deoradhan,
"descendant of the exiled one."

DUAIBSEACH f. (duav-suk) "sad, sorrowful, melancholy." An early regal name.

DUARCÁN m. (duar-cawn) From *duairc*, "sad, melancholy." Anglicized Durcan or Dorcan.

ÉIGEARTACH m. (ayg-art-ock) "wrongdoer, unjust person." An early name from the south. From it derives the
contemporary surname O'Hegarty (O hÉigeartach).

ETAIN/Étaín/Éadaoin/Etaoin f. (ed-en or ay-deen) Thought to be derived from *ét*, "jealousy." Perhaps a name for a sun goddess in earliest times, there is also at least one saint recorded with the name. It occurs in several stories, the most remarkable of which, Tochmar Étaíne, "The Wooing of Etain," names Etain as one of the fairy folk of Ireland, the Tuatha Dé Dannan. A jealous rival transforms Etain into a scarlet fly and causes her to be blown by winds all over Ireland. After fourteen years of this rough treatment, the fly falls into a cup and is consumed by a warrior's wife, who becomes pregnant. Thus Etain is reborn. *The Immortal Hour,* an opera of 1914 by Rutland Boughton, is based on this tale. The form Aideen is a popular contemporary Anglicization.

FACHTNA f. & m. (fokt-na) "malicious, hostile." A relatively commonly used early name, for men rather than women. The name is borne by four saints, the most notable of which established a monastery in the sixth century at Rosscarbery, County Cork. Fachnan and Faughnan are variant forms, and it is rendered as Festus and Festie among the O'Mores and the O'Farrells and Latinized as Fantasius, no less.

FANN/Fand f. (fon, fown) A name connected with the Old Irish word *fand,* "a tear." In Irish mythology, Fand was wife to the sea god, Manannán mac Lir.

FIONGHUINE/Finguine m. (f'un-in-e) "kin slayer." Strangely, a popular early name.

FÓGARTA/Fócarta n. (foeg-art-a) "one who is proclaimed an outlaw."

GRAINNE/Gráinne/Grania f. (graw-nya) A name that might be interpreted as "she who inspires terror" as well as being connected with the word *grán*, "grain." Grainne is the name of one of the preeminent mythological women of Ireland. Daughter of the high king, Cormac Mac Art, and betrothed against her will to Finn Mac Cool, she eloped with Dermot, one of Finn's soldiers, commencing a sixteen-year hunt throughout the country for the lovers. Megalithic sites throughout Ireland are still traditionally referred to as Dermot and Grania's bed. The name retained its prominence in the historical personage of Gráinne Ní Mháille (d.1600) the successful pirate leader of the seafaring O'Malleys. Her name was Anglicized Grace O'Malley, and she became a poetic symbol for Ireland. Grace is an arbitrary translation of the name, Grania being the acceptable form.

GÚASACHT m. (guas-ocht) "danger, peril." The name of a saint, Saint Gúasacht of Granard.

KENNEDY/Cinnéide/Cennétig f. & m. "ugly-headed, rough-headed," as well as perhaps "helmet-headed." Cennétig mac Lorcain was the father of Brian Boru. Principally a surname, it is finding increasing favor now as a first name for both boys and girls.

MAOLANAITHE m. (mel-an-a-ha) "devotee of the storm." A saint's name.

REAGAN/Regan f. & m. From the Irish surname, it may be variously interpreted as connected with *ri*, "king," or *riodhgach*, "impulsive, furious."

SCANNAL/Scandal m. (skon-al) From the Irish *scandal*, "quarrel, contention."

SIADHAL m. (sheel) A name borne by two saints. From *siadhail,* "sloth."

SÍLE/Sheila f. This the Irish form of the Latin Cecilia, itself a female form of Cecil, which is derived from *caecus,* "blind." The name was brought to Ireland by the Anglo-Normans and has been used popularly since. Shelagh, Sheelagh, Shilla, Selia, Shela, Shelia, Shiela, and Sheelah are just some of the variant spellings that have emerged throughout Britain, Australia, and America, along with contemporary forms in the United States such as Shahla and Shayla. Saint Cecilia, the patron saint of music, has long been romanticized as a popular subject by painters and writers.

TASSACH m. (tos-ach) "idle, inactive." Legend has it that Tassach was the bishop who gave Saint Patrick the last rites.

TÉIDE f. (tay-de) "wantonness." In legend, Téide was one of the wives of Finn.

TORNA m. "puffed up." In early legend, Torna Eces appears as a learned scholar.

UNCHI f. "contention."

Banshee

Banshee is a term that derives from the Irish *bean sídhe,* "fairy woman." The fairy people, or Daoine Sídhe (deeny shee), were in folklore believed to be the original inhabitants of the land. They were magical and powerful and could cause great trouble for anyone who disrespected them. Sometimes they were capricious and cruel for their own sport. Many old families invoked a bean sídhe as a patroness of their lineage, to promote their social status and discourage interference from other fairy mischief. The folk tradition of the wailing of the banshee as a warning to the family that a member will soon die is well-known. In this instance, they were originally deemed to be acting as guardians, heralds of tribulation to come, and not, as the popular contemporary perception holds, as malicious agents of doom. The following names are those that have been associated in folk tradition with particular fairy women.

ÁINE f. (awn-ye) This name comes from early times in Ireland, and not surprisingly, carries a wealth of pagan lore with it. As well as being the name of an early goddess, Áine was later known to be a banshee of the northern family O'Corr, and in the south as a patroness of the Norman family, Fitzgerald.

BEVIN/Béibhinn/Bébinn f. In folklore, Bevin was a giantess and daughter of the king of the Otherworld. She left her husband Aodh Álainn and sought the protection of Finn Mac Cool. Sadly, her jealous husband succeeded in killing her and she was buried by the Fianna with great ceremony.

CLIONA/Clíodhna Cliona was claimed as fairy patroness by the MacCarthy family of the south. In stories, she appears as a lady who suffers the loss of her lover and also as a young woman who took many lovers. She was also, as a muse, regularly invoked by poets.

MINIVER f. This name is really Welsh in origin. Its early use occurs in Cornwall where it appears to be a regional form of the name Guinevere, "fair and smooth." In Cornwall there is a story of Saint Miniver who, while combing her hair beside a well, was tempted by the devil himself. She responded by throwing her comb at him, and he was forced to change into a stone to avoid being hit. In Irish folklore, sometimes the banshee is combing her hair while wailing. If she should throw her comb at someone and it strikes them, then that person will die within the space of a triad, whether it be days, months, or years.

NIAMH f. (nee-av) Niamh was variously a fairy woman and a femme fatale in Irish legend. Celtchair Mac Cuthacair (kelcher mac cuh-acar) married off his daughter, Niamh, to his invincible rival, Conganchas Mac Daire (kung-anas mac dawra), in order that she might discover his weakness. Niamh reveals to her father that her husband can only be slain by spearing the soles of his feet and the calves of his legs. In due course, Conganchas is slain. In another story, Niamh incites Oisín to his first battle. Most famously, Niamh Chinn Oír seduces Oisín and takes him off to Tir na nÓg, from whence he returns 300 years later to find the old heroic age in Ireland to have passed.

SCATHACH f. (skaw-hoch) Most famously, Scathach appears as a fairy woman who instructs the young hero Cúchulainn in the use of weapons. Her name may be connected with the island of Skye, off the coast of Scotland. In the Finn tales, Scathach appears in gentler guise, lulling Finn to sleep in a fairy mound with the use of magical music.

UNA f. (oon-a) Una was claimed as the fairy patroness, bean sídhe, of the O'Carroll family.

Fancies

Ireland has been no slouch in the production-of-writers department. And authors will invent names for their heroes and heroines. The following short list recalls some of the more notable examples of authorial license and discovers a few names that became singularly successful thereafter. Some of these names have current appeal, some are merely curiosities. The trend for developing new names or hybrids of a few older names is presently quite strong, especially in the United States. This group of names reminds us that all names have to be born somewhere.

CASPIAN m. A name borrowed from the sea of the same title by C. S. Lewis, the Northern Irish author of the popular children's books *The Chronicles of Narnia*. Fanciful, but useful.

FIONA f. This name was originally invented by the Scots eighteenth-century author James Macpherson, probably as a feminine form of the heroic name Fionn. It was popularized by another author, also a Scot, William Sharp, who used the pen name Fiona Macleod, writing Celtic romantic sagas in the nineteenth century. The name is popularly used throughout the British Isles. In Ireland, use of Fiona is probably connected with the older name Fina, "vine," which can be written Fíona in contemporary Irish.

GLORIA f. The Latin word for "glory" was first used as a woman's name by the playwright George Bernard Shaw for one his characters in *You Never Can Tell* (1898). It has been well used since, rising to a popular peak in the United States during the 1950s.

GULLIVER m. A name invented by Jonathan Swift (1667–1745), Dublin-born author and satirist, for the hero of his fantastic work, *Gulliver's Travels.* The name is really a surname, the biblical name Lemuel ("devoted to God") being Gulliver's first name, but there seems little reason why it should not be deployed today as a first name.

IMOGEN f. This name has been adopted from Shakespeare's play, *Cymbeline.* Curiously, the spelling Imogen occurs possibly as an error, as the source used by Shakespeare lists the name as Innogen, a name that probably has roots in the Gaelic *inighion,* meaning "daughter."

INEENDUV f. This name derives from Scots Gaelic Ineen Duv, which is rendered in Irish as Iníon Dubh, "dark daughter." The name was a title used popularly for Finola MacDonnell, daughter of a Scots highland chief and mother of the rebel Earl of Tyrconnell, Red Hugh O'Donnell (d.1602).

JUNO f. Use of the Latin name of the queen of the gods by playwright Sean O'Casey for his character in the play, *Juno* *and the Paycock.* It is most likely an elaboration on the Irish name Una, and contrary to the impression given by the play, was probably not employed as a name by Irish parents.

MALVINA f. An invention of the eighteenth-century author James Macpherson, who used the name in his popular fictional work, *Ossian*, a series of heroic verses, which was also responsible for spreading the name Oscar widely throughout Europe.

ORINTHIA f. Another invention of George Bernard Shaw's, in his play *The Apple Cart.* It may derive from the male name Oran or the feminine name Orna.

VANESSA f. Jonathan Swift also invented this name in his poem "Cadenus and Vanessa." The name is a partial anagram of the name of Esther Vanhomrigh, a lady who was somewhat keen on the author but whom Swift wished to discourage in verse without being cruel. In the twentieth century, the name has been well used in the English-speaking world, especially in recent decades in the United States.

Translations

§ The use of Irish names over the past 1,000 years reflects the varied history of conquest and settlement that has occurred on this relatively small island. Early Celtic civilization had to make room for, in succession, the Vikings, the Normans, and the English. Residual influence from all of these periods has strongly colored Irish society, and obviously, Irish names. Additionally, as Christianity took hold in Ireland, rising to become an important source of power and influence at home and abroad, name choices reflected the change. The warlike names of old—Aichear, Buach, Mocha—yielded to peace-loving names favored by the clergy—Colm, Maol Mhuire, Mannix. People were named less frequently for great warriors of the past and more often for Christian inspirational figures.

Throughout these times, there were particular Irish ways of pronouncing and spelling the imported new names. The Scandinavian name Olaf became Auliffe; the French Norman name Jeanette became Sinead; and the Anglo-Norman form Thomas became Tomás. In the specific instance of English colonization—a process that began sporadically in the twelfth century but took on a structured and ruthless form in the sixteenth century—strange alliances between names occured. Under Henry VIII the native Irish people were disqualified from owning land and were severely pressured to adopt the English language and convert to the Anglican church. In the systematic and ruthless oppression that followed throughout the next centuries, Anglicization became the norm. Irish names were converted to Anglophonic forms, translated, and associated with names they bore no relationship with. Women with the name Gormlaith were compelled to adopt the name Barbara. Gobnets became Deborahs or Abigails. Aodh was changed to Hugh, Diarmaid to Jeremiah or Dermot. This process continued until, by the beginning of the twentieth century, Irish names with an original Irish form were all but extinct in Ireland itself.

With the emergence of hard-won nationhood in 1921, there came a reawakened interest in traditional Irish culture. In 1923, Father Patrick Woulfe published *Irish Names for Children,* a text he hoped would encourage parents to opt for Irish names rather than the imported fashionable names of the moment: John and Mary were the most popular names for children at that time. Slowly, but surely, Woulfe's hope began to be realized, and Irish names started to come back into use. It is possible to see the contemporary usage of earlier Irish name forms as a continuation of this ongoing restoration and reappraisal by the Irish of their own culture. Of course, the winds of fashion have continued to promote, and indeed favor, use of Anglophonic names in Ireland, but there is a healthy representation of traditional Irish names very much in evidence today.

Another chapter in this story arises from the retranslation back into Irish of popularly used Anglophonic names. Nationalist educators pushed for a process of converting Anglo names into Irish equivalents or into freshly minted Irish forms. In this way, people who bore the name John were encouraged to adopt the form Sean or Eoin; people who bore the name Mary were encouraged to use the form Máire. When I was in school, boys with the name Francis had to respond to the name Proinsias, and girls with the name Deborah vexedly had to answer to the name Gobnet. My own surname, Johnson, was translated into either MacSean or MacEoin, both technically correct, depending which teacher I had. Contemporary Irish did not, it seems, embrace all the older forms. The name Desmond, for instance, is an Anglicized form of the old Irish name Desmumhnach (das-oon-ach), meaning "man of Mumhain." In the retranslation process, Desmond became Deasún (das-oon), a new coinage.

Perhaps these instances go some way toward unraveling the various conditions and influences that have been brought to bear in the history of Irish nomenclature. Without wishing to compound the confusion, the following lists are examples of Anglicized Irish names and Irishized English names popularly used during these periods.

English Names and Irish Translations

Aaron	*to*	Árón (ar-awn) m.
Abbie	*to*	Abaigh (ab-ee) f.
Abigail	*to*	Abaigeal (abi-gyal) *f* .
Adam	*to*	Ádhamh or Ádam (aw-hav or aw-dam) m.
Adrian	*to*	Aidrian m.
Agatha	*to*	Ágata (ogata) f.
Agnes	*to*	Aignéis (ayg-nesh) f.
Alan	*to*	Ailín (ayl-en) m.
Alexander	*to*	Alsander m.
Alexandra	*to*	Alastríona (alus-treena) f.
Alfred	*to*	Ailfrid (ayl-frid) m.
Alice	*to*	Ailís (ay-leesh) f.
Alicia	*to*	Ailíse (ay-leesha) f.
Amelia	*to*	Aimilíona (amil-eeona) f.

Anastasia	*to*	Ánnstas (on-stews) f.
Andrew	*to*	Aindréas or Aindriú or Aindrias (endrace, en-dru, or en-dreeas) m.
Angela	*to*	Aingeal (angell) f.
Anne, Anna	*to*	Ánna (onna) f.
Arthur	*to*	Artúr (ar-toor) m.
Augustine	*to*	Ághuistín or Aibhistín (aw-ghush-teen or awv-ishteen) m.
Austin	*to*	Oistín (ish-teen) m.
Barbara	*to*	Bairbre with pet form Baibin (ba-been) f.
Barnaby	*to*	Barnaib (bar-nab) m.
Bernard	*to*	Bearnárd (bar-nard) m.
Catherine	*to*	Caitrín or Caitríona or Caitlín (cot-reen, cot-reeona, or cotch-leen) with pet forms Cáit or Triona (cawtch or treeona) f.
Cecily	*to*	Síle (sheila) f.
Charles	*to*	Searlas or Carlus (shar-lus or car-lus) m.
Charlotte	*to*	Searlait (shar-lat) f.
Christina	*to*	Crístíona (cree-steeona) f.
Christopher	*to*	Criostóir (kris-tour) with Christie or Christy as pet forms m.
Colin	*to*	Coilín or Coileán (kil-een or kil-awn) m.
David	*to*	Daibhi or Daibhead or Daithi (daw-vee, daw-vade, or daw-hee) m.
Edmund	*to*	Eamonn (ay-mon) m.
Edna	*to*	Eithne (eth-na) f.
Edward	*to*	Éadbhárd (ayad-vard) m.
Edwina	*to*	Éadeoin (aye-din) f.
Eleanor	*to*	Eileanóra or Eileanóir or Ailionóra (elanora, elanor, or ayl-inora) f.
Elizabeth	*to*	Eilís (i-leesh) f.
Emily	*to*	Eimíle (em-eela) f.

Esther	to	Eistir (esh-tir) f.
Eustace	to	Iustás (yoo-staws) m.
Eva	to	Eábha (aya-va) f.
Frances	to	Proinséas (proon-shas) f.
Francis	to	Proinsias (proon-she-as) m.
Gareth	to	Gairiad (gar-iad) m.
Geoffrey	to	Siothrún or Seathrún (shuh-rune or shah-rune) or in pet form, Sheary (shah-ree) m.
George	to	Seoirse (shor-she) m.
Gerald	to	Gearóid (gar-ode) m.
Gerard	to	Gearárd or Gearóid (jer-ord or gar-ode) m.
Godfrey	to	Gofraidh (gu-free) m.
Graham	to	Gréachán (gray-hawn) m.
Gregory	to	Gréagóir or Greagoir (gray-agore or greg-ore) m.
Harold	to	Aralt (ar-olt) m.
Helen, Helena	to	Léan or Leána (lay-an or lay-ana)
Henry	to	Anraí or Annraoi (on-ree) m.
Herbert	to	Hoireabard (ir-abard) m.
Hilary	to	Hiolaír (heel-ore) f.
Hubert	to	Hoibeard (hib-eard) m.
Isaac	to	Íosac (ee-osac) m.
Isabel	to	Isibéal or Sibéal (ish-bayl or shi-bayl) f.
Ivor	to	Íomhar (ee-ovar) m.
James	to	Séamas or Seumas or Seamus (shay-mus) or as pet form, Shay m.
Jamie	to	Séimí (shay-mee) m.
Jane	to	Síne (sheena) f.
Janet	to	Sinéad (shin-ade) f.
Joan	to	Siobhán (shiv-aun) f.
John	to	Seán or Eoin (shaun or owen) m.
Jonathan	to	Ionatán (yo-nat-aun) m.
Joseph	to	Seosamh or Íoseph (sho-saf or yo-saf) m.

Josephine	*to*	Seosamhín (sho-safeen) f.
Julia	*to*	Iúile (yu-le) f.
Kate	*to*	Cáit (cawtch) f.
Laurence	*to*	Labhrás (law-raws) m.
Leo	*to*	León (lee-own) m.
Lily	*to*	Líle (lee-le) f.
Louise	*to*	Labhaoise (law-eeshe) f.
Luke	*to*	Lucás (luc-aws) m.
Mable	*to*	Máible (maw-bile) f.
Madeleine	*to*	Madailéin (mada-lane) f.
Marcel	*to*	Mairsile (mar-sheel) m.
Marcella	*to*	Mairsile (mar-sheel) f.
Margaret	*to*	Mairghread or Mairéad (mar-ade or mor-ade) f.
Mark	*to*	Marcus or Marcas m.
Martha	*to*	Marta f.
Martin	*to*	Máirtín, or Martán (mar-cheen or mor-taun) m.
Mary	*to*	Máire (moyra) or Moira or Maura or Máirín (mau-reen) f.
Matilda	*to*	Maitilde (mat-ilde) f.
Matthew	*to*	Maitú or Matha (mat-yoo, or mot-a) m.
Maud	*to*	Máda (maud-a) f.
Maurice	*to*	Muiris (mwi-rish) m.
Michael	*to*	Micheál or Míchaél (me-haul or me-hale) m.
Monica	*to*	Moncha (mun-cha) f.
Nancy	*to*	Nainsí (nan-shee) f.
Nell	*to*	Neile (nay-le) f.
Nicholas	*to*	Nioclás (neec-laws) m.
Oliver	*to*	Oilibhear (oliv-are) m.
Patricia	*to*	Pádraigín (paud-rigeen) f.
Patrick	*to*	Pádraig or Pádraic or Pádhraic (paw-rig or pawd-rig), with pet forms Páid, Páidín, Páidí, or Padhra (pawj, paw-jean, pawjee, or parra) m.

Paul	*to*	Pól (pole) m.
Pauline	*to*	Póilín (pole-een) f.
Peter	*to*	Peadar (pa-ther) m.
Philip	*to*	Pilib (fil-ib) m.
Piers	*to*	Feoras (fee-oras) or Piaras (peer-ash) m.
Polly	*to*	Paili (polly) f.
Rachel	*to*	Ráichéal (raw-shale) f.
Ralph	*to*	Rádhulbh (roh-ulf) m.
Randolph	*to*	Ronnulbh (ron-ulf) m.
Raymond	*to*	Réamann (reay-man) or Redmond m.
Richard	*to*	Ristéard or Riocard (reesh-teard or reec-ord) m.
Robert	*to*	Roibéard (row-beard) m.
Roland	*to*	Rolann (row-lan) m.
Rolf	*to*	Rodhulbh (row-ulf) m.
Rose	*to*	Róis (rowsh) f.
Ruth	*to*	Rut (root) f.
Simon	*to*	Síomón (she-mone) m.
Stacey	*to*	Stéise (stay-sha) f.
Stephen	*to*	Stiofán (sti-fawn) m.
Susan	*to*	Súsanna (soo-sana) with pet form Siuí (su-ee) f.
Theresa	*to*	Toiréasa or Treasa (tir-aysa or trassa) f.
Thomas	*to*	Tomás (to-maws) m.
Valentine	*to*	Bhailintín (val-enteen) m.
Vincent	*to*	Uinsean (in-shan) m.
Walter	*to*	Ualtar (oohl-tar) m.
William	*to*	Uilliam or Liam (oohl-yam or lee-am) m.

IRISH NAMES AND ENGLISH TRANSLATIONS

| Aengus/ Aonghus | *to* | Aeneas or Enos or Nicholas m. |
| Ailbe/Alby | *to* | Albert or Bertie m. |

Ailbhe/Alby/

Elva	*to*	Olive f.
Áine	*to*	Anne or Anna or Hannah f.

Aisling/

Aislinn	*to*	Alice or Esther f.
Almha	*to*	Alva f.

Anéislis/

Aneslis	*to*	Standish or Stanislaus m.
Aodh	*to*	Hugh or Eugene m.
Aoife	*to*	Eva f.
Ardgal/Ardal	*to*	Arnold m.
Art	*to*	Arthur m.
Auliffe	*to*	Humphrey m.
Béibhinn	*to*	Vivian f.
Bláthnait	*to*	Flora or Florence f.
Blinne	*to*	Blanche f.
Breasal	*to*	Basil m.
Brian	*to*	Bernard or Barnaby or Barney m.

Cahir/

Cathair	*to*	Charles m.

Calbhach/

Calvagh	*to*	Charles m.

Canice/

Cainneach	*to*	Kenneth or Kenny m.
Cathal	*to*	Charles m.
Cearbhall	*to*	Charles or Carroll m.

Conchobhar/

Conor	*to*	Cornelius or Corney m.
Conn	*to*	Constantine m.
Cormac	*to*	Charles m.
Cúmhaí	*to*	Hughey or Quinton m.
Dara	*to*	Dudley m.
Diarmaid/		Jeremiah or Jerome or Jeremy or Darby
Dermot	*to*	m.
Doireann	*to*	Doreen or Dorothy or Dolly f.
Donal	*to*	Daniel m.

Donnchadh/

Donagh	*to*	Dennis or Dionysus m.

Dubhaltach	*to*	Dudley m.
Earnan	*to*	Ernest m.
Eíbhear	*to*	Harry or Heber or Ivor or Irving m.
Eígneachan/		
Eneas	*to*	Ignatius or Aeneas m.
Eímhean	*to*	Evan m.
Eireamhon	*to*	Hermon or Irwin m.
Eithne	*to*	Annie or Anna f.
Eoghan	*to*	Eugene or Owen m.
Fachtna	*to*	Festus or Fantasius m.
Fainche	*to*	Fanny f.
Fearadhach	*to*	Ferdinand or Frederick m.
Fechin	*to*	Festus m.
Fergus	*to*	Ferdinand m.
Fiach	*to*	Festus m.
Fineen	*to*	Florence or Florry or Flurry m.
Finola/		
Fionnuala	*to*	Flora or Penelope f.
Flann	*to*	Florence f. & m.
Giolla Chríst/		
Gilchrist	*to*	Christian m.
Gobnet/		
Gobnait	*to*	Deborah or Abigail or Abbie or Dora f.
Gormlaith	*to*	Barbara f.
Gráinne/		
Grania	*to*	Grace or Gertrude or Griselda f.
Honor/Onóra	*to*	Hannah f.
Lachtna	*to*	Lucius m.
Laoiseach	*to*	Louis or Lewis or Lucius m.
Lasairian	*to*	Lazarus m.
Lochlainn	*to*	Laurence m.
Lorcan	*to*	Laurence m.
Lughaidh	*to*	Louis or Lewis or Aloysius m.
Luiseach	*to*	Lucy f.
Maelea- chlainn	*to*	Malachy m.
Mael- maodhog	*to*	Malachy m.

Maeve		Mabel or Madge or Maude or Marjory
	to	f.
Maille	*to*	Molly f.
Maolbhean-		
nachta	*to*	Benedict m.
Maolmhuire	*to*	Milo or Myles or Murray m.
Maolíosa	*to*	Melissa f.
Mór	*to*	Martha or Mary or Agatha f.
Muadhnait	*to*	Mona f.
Muireann	*to*	Marion or Madge f.
Murtagh/		
Muir-		
cheartach	*to*	Mortimer or Maurice m.
Naoise	*to*	Noah m.
Niall	*to*	Nicholas or Nigel m.
Nora	*to*	Daisy f.
Nuala	*to*	Penelope or Penny f.
Phelim/		
Feidhlim	*to*	Felix m.
Raghnailt	*to*	Regina f.
Ríona	*to*	Regina f.
Rory/Ruairí	*to*	Roderick or Richard or Roger m.
Saraid	*to*	Sarah f.
Seanán/		
Senan	*to*	Simon m.
Sheila/Síle	*to*	Judith or Judy or Julia f.
Siobhán		Joan or Judith or Judy or Julia or
	to	Hannah or Susan or Susannah f.
Sive/Sadhbh	*to*	Sarah or Sabia or Sally or Sophia f.
Sorcha	*to*	Sally or Sarah f.
Suibhne	*to*	Simon m.
Tadhg		Timothy or Thaddeus or Ted or Toby
	to	m.
Turlough	*to*	Charles m.
Uaithne	*to*	Anthony or Hewney m.
Una	*to*	Agnes or Unity or Winifred or Juno f.

A to Z

ADAMNAN/Adhamhnán/Adomnán m. (ay-on-awn) Traditionally, this name is thought to be an Irish pet form of the biblical name Adam (Ádhamh), but current scholarship suggests that it is an older name with a meaning like "timid one." Saint Adamnan was a seventh-century abbot of some influence who wrote an early record of the life of Saint Columba and is the first scribe to make reference to the Loch Ness Monster. The name was Anglicized Eunan and transcribed also as Awnan, Ounan, Junan, and Junanan.

AENGUS/Aonghus/Óengus/Aonghas m. (eng-us) Aengus was one of the early Irish divinities, a god of youth and love. His name may be interpreted as "one choice" or "true vigor," and in writing he is referred to as Aengus Óg ("the young"). He was an aid to lovers, notably Dermot and Grania, and suffered himself on account of love. Kings, warriors, and poets have borne the name, as well as five saints of record. In Scotland, the name takes on the more familiar form, Angus.

AIFRIC/Affraic/Africa f. (af-ric) Opinions differ as to whether this name, borne by two abbesses of Kildare in the eighth and ninth centuries, is a borrowing of the name Africa, after the continent, or a genuinely Gaelic name deriving from a word for "pleasant." One lady named Africa was betrothed to a twelfth-century monarch of the Isle of Man.

AILEEN/Aibhílín f. (ay-leen) This is an Irish form of the Norman name Evelyn, currently very popular in Ireland, where it has replaced the earlier favorite form, Eileen. In the past, it has also been used as an Irish equivalent of Helen. Ailine, Ailene, and Ailleen are other spellings used in the United States.

AILILL/Oilill m. (al-il) "a sprite, an elf." An early Irish name, at one time among the most popularly used names for men, all but defunct today. It occurs in the tales of Finn and the Fianna, and was used by royalty and clergy. Two saints of record bore the name. Aillen (al-len) and Oillin (ul-een) are diminutives.

AILISH/Ailís f. (ay-lish) An Irish form of the Norman name Alice, "noble." In the past, the name was also used more loosely as a translation for Elizabeth. Ailíse is the form used for Alicia.

AINDRIAS/Aindreas m. (an-dree-as) An Irish form of Andrew, "manly."

AINGEAL f. (ang-ell) An Irish form of Angela, "angel."

AISLINN/Aisling/Ashling f. (ash-ling) "a vision, a dream." Rarely used as a name in earlier times, it has been widely popular in Ireland since the last century, possibly in part due to its use as a name for a particular form of poetic composition—the evocation of Ireland in the persona of a beautiful woman. A nice Irish counterpoint to the phonetically similar, currently red-hot Ashley. Ashlinn, Ashlyn, and Ashlynn are forms found in the United States.

ALANNAH/Alana/Allana f. (al-anna) Though this may be interpreted as a feminine form of Alan, it is likely that the Gaelic endearment *a leanbh,* meaning "O child," has had more to do with its continued use as a name in Ireland.

ALASTAR m. (alus-tur) The Irish form of Alexander, "defender of men." As Alastair, the name was especially popular in Scotland, and it occurs also as Alasdair, Alistair, Alusdar, and Alusdrann.

ALASTRÍONA/Alastrina f. (alus-treena) An Irish form of Alexandra.

ALVA/Almha f. Almha was a member of the mythical tribe of divinities called the Tuatha Dé Danann (tu-aha day danan), "people of the goddess Dana," the legendary forbears of the Irish. The fortress and hill at Almu in Leinster are named for her.

ANESLIS/Ainéislis m. (an-ash-lis) A name used in the early Middle Ages, "careful, thoughtful." It was Anglicized, strangely, as the Slavonic name Stanislaus, and Standish is a further pet form.

ARDAL/Ardghal/Ardgal m. (ar-dal) "high valour," an old name that may have its origins in the earlier name Art.

ATTRACTA f. (a-trackta) This exotic name was borne by a sixth-century saint from Sligo, for whom Killaraght, where she founded her nunnery, was named. Though used sparingly, the name is still found today.

AULIFFE/Amhlaoibh m. (aw-liv) This is an Irish form of the Viking name Olaf, "heir to his ancestors." Later Anglicized as Humphrey, an unconnected name.

AWLEY/Amhalgaidh m. (aw-lee) A very early name with regal associations originating in the southwest of the country. Auley is another possible Anglicization.

BANBA/Banbha f. (ban-vah) Banba was an early Irish goddess whose name was given to the plain of Meath and later to the country as a whole. Folklore tells of the three sister goddesses, Banba, Fodla (foe-lah) and Éire (ear-ah) who vied with settlers to have the land named after them. Éire was the eventual victor, though Banba and Fodla are used as poetic evocations of Ireland.

BEANÓN/Benen/Beineóin m. (ban-own) An Irish translation of the Latin name Benignus, "mild," given by Saint Patrick to a favorite disciple.

BEATHA/Betha f. (ba-ha or beh-tha) From *beatha,* "life." The male name Mac Beatha means "son of life," and gives the surname, and the name of Shakespeare's "Scottish play," *Macbeth.*

BECAN/Beacán m. (bec-awn) "little man." Occurs as a pet form of Beag or Bec, "little," a name used originally for both sexes.

BENVON/Bean Mhumhan f. Bean Mhumhain (ban-vune) Means "Lady of Munster." A name was in use up until the seventeenth century. Benvon is a somewhat clumsy Anglicization.

BENVY/Bean Mhí f. Bean Mhí (ban-vee) Means "Lady of Meath." This was a popular name up until the seventeenth century among the O'Connors, MacMahons, and O'Neils. Benvy is a less than glamorous Anglicization.

BERNADETTE f. An imported French name used widely in Ireland in the early part of this century in honor of Saint Bernadette Soubirous (1844–1879) whose visions of the Virgin Mary at Lourdes caused a sensation in the Catholic church. Bernadetta and Bernadine have also been recorded. Berna, Bernie, and Detta are shortened forms.

BIDDY/Biddie f. A pet form of Brigid, once so commonly used that it became a bi-word for any Irish woman. Contemporary associations, along with such expressions as "an old biddy," are less kind to the name, which is now almost unused.

BIDELIA/Bedelia f. This name, and Bedina, are elaborate forms of Biddy. Shortened versions gave rise to Delia, Dillie, and Dina. Along with Biddy, they have suffered a severe drop in usage and are commonly perceived as part of a bygone era.

BLINNE f. (blin-neh) This is a later form used for the name Moninne, the name of a saint of the sixth century who was supposed to have been friendly with the two great Irish patron saints, Patrick and Brigid. Blinne was Anglicized as Blanche.

BRADY m. The Irish surname used as a first name, usually in the United States or Australia. Bradie is another recorded form.

BRANDON m. The use of this name in Ireland derives from the name Brendan. The feast of Saint Brendan on May 16 is marked by an annual pilgrimage to the summit of Mount Brandon in County Kerry. The name exists also as an English surname meaning "gorse hill." Currently very popular in the United States, where it also appears as Branden, Brandin, and Brandyn.

BREE f. It is not clear whether this name is an individual name from a similar root, or another form of the name Brigid. Either way, it is a name indicating divinity, meaning "exalted one." It occurs as an element in names such as Breeanne and Breeanna, currently well used in the United States.

BRENDAN/Breandán m. A name originating from a Welsh word, *breenhin,* meaning prince. This was rendered as Breanainn in old Irish, and transcribed as Brendanus in Latin, from whence the current forms Brendan and Breandán (brandawn). Well used since its formulation, some seventeen saints are said to have held the name, the most famous of whom, Saint Brendan of Clonfert (484–577), was also known as Saint Brendan the Navigator who was believed to have crossed the Atlantic and whose account of his journey was translated into seven different languages. Brenden and Brendon are alternate forms found in the United States.

BRIAN m. Opinion is divided as to the origin and meaning of this name. It is thought to be Celtic in origin, but it is not clear which Celtic language introduced it. In Irish, it first occurred as Brion (bree-on), thought to mean "high, noble." In this early form, it was widely used, but it became most famous in its later form through the figure of Brian Boru (926–1014), the high king who brought unity to the warring dynasties and who successfully broke the Viking hold on the country at the battle of Clontarf, where he was eventually slain. Widely used throughout the English-speaking world, variable forms include Bryan, Bryant, Bryon, Briano and, in contemporary Irish, Briain (bree-on).

BRIANNA f. A modern feminine form of Brian, especially popular in Canada and the United States. Briana, Bryanna, Bryana, and Brianne are variants.

BRIGID/Brighid f. An early name for a goddess revered throughout the Celtic world. Brighid (breed) means "the exalted one" or "the high goddess," a divinity associated with fire, agriculture, and poetry. Some fifteen saints are said to have borne the name, but they are all easily eclipsed by the reputation of Saint Brigid of Kildare, who in folklore seems to have taken on many of the properties and powers of her older pagan namesake. In reverence to Saint Brigid, the name did not come into common usage in Ireland until the eighteenth century, becoming then wildly popular, eventually being used as a generic name for an Irish woman. Anglicized as Bridget or Briget, it became entangled with the Swedish form of the name, Birgitta or Brigitta, borne by that country's patron saint, whose feast day falls coincidentally on the same day as Saint Brigid of Kildare's, February 1. The popular forms that ensued include Bríd (breed), Bride, Bridie, Bridin (bree-jean), Bridgeteen, Breege, Breda, Breeda, Bree, Brigitte, Birgit, Brigida, Biddy, Biddle, Bid, and Beesy.

CADHLA/Cadla m. (kay-la) "beautiful, comely," an old name originating in the south, from whence we get the surname O Cadhla, which is Angicized as Kiely. To a modern ear, the name perhaps sounds more suited as a girl's name, Kayleigh, Keighley, and the currently red-hot Kayla being contemporary favorite examples.

CAIRBRE m. (car-bre) A name that occurs frequently in legend, and one of the most popular male names in early Ireland. Distinguished leaders such as Cormac Mac Art and Niall of the Nine Hostages gave this name to their sons. Carbery is an Anglicized form, and Carbury in County Kildare reflects another spelling.

CAIRENN/Caireann f. (kar-en) Thought to be an early borrowing of the Latin name Carina, "dear one," this was the name of the mother of the great warrior, Niall of the Nine Hostages, ancestor to the high kings of Ireland.

CAITLIN/Caitlín f. (koit-leen or kotch-leen) This is an Irish form of Catherine, taken from the Norman French version, Cateline. In Ireland, the name proved popular and gave the Anglicized forms Kathleen and Cathleen, both widely used in the English speaking world. In the United States, the old form of the name persisted in popularity, and still shows great staying power, but took on a different pronunciation, which is reflected in the contemporary spellings: Kaitlyn, Katelyn(n), Kaytlin, Cathline, Katelin, Kateline, Kaitlin, and Caitlyn(n).

CALBHACH/Calvach m. (col-vak) "bald." A popular name in the later Middle Ages that echoes the Latin-originated name Calvin, which has the same meaning. Calvagh is an Anglicized form.

CALLAGHAN m. From Ceallachán, a pet form of Ceallach (Kelly), hence, perhaps, "little Kelly." As Ceallachan, the name was borne by an early king of Munster. Today it is more usually found as a surname.

CANICE/Cainneach m. (can-is or kin-noch) "pleasant person." Saint Canice was a sixth-century missionary who founded churches in Wales, Scotland, and Ireland. Canicus was the Latin translation of his name, from which derives the English form, Canice. The name is also rendered as Kelly and Kenneth in place names that were named for him, notably Killkenny and Inchkenneth.

CAOILTE m. (keel-cha) One possible root for this name is "hard," but its meaning is uncertain. In legend, Caoilte was a relative of Finn Mac Cool and was noted for his swiftness of foot.

CAOIMHE f. (keev-ah) "precious, beloved, graceful." From old Irish *caem*. Keavy is a clumsy Anglicization; perhaps the phonetic spelling, Keevah, would be more true to the source.

CAOLÁN m. (kway-lawn or kay-lawn) "slender lad." The name of two saints of record. Anglicized Kelan or Kealan.

CAOMH/Caem m. (keev) "precious, beloved, beautiful." Many older names begin with the root *caem*, including Kevin (Caoimhín), Caoimhe, and Caoimhinn. From it derives the contemporary surname, O'Keefe. As it is, Caomh seems admirably simple to a contemporary ear, and suitable for a girl or a boy.

CARRAIG/Carrig m. (car-ig) From Irish *carraig,* "rock." Carrick is the Scots Gaelic form. Craig is the most commonly used form from this Gaelic root.

CARTHACH/Cartagh m. (kor-huk) From this name, in the personage of Carthach Mac Sáirbrethaig (mac sor-bre-hig), evolved the surname MacCarthy, the powerful family that dominated the southwest of Ireland. Two saints of note bore the name. Carthy is another form it took, and it was Anglicized as Carthage.

CAS/Cass f. & m. This name means "curly-haired" and was a relatively common name for men in the early period. The early tribe known as the Dal Cais were called after an ancestor of this name. From it stems the surname Cassidy. Cassán (cass-awn) is a pet form.

CATRIONA f. (ka-tree-ona) This is an Irish form of Catherine that derives from an older Greek name meaning "pure." The name also occurs as Catrina, and in shortened form as Triona, Trina, and Traoine. The name is well-used in Ireland and in Scotland, where it also takes the form Caitríona.

CAVAN/Cabhan m. From the place name Cavan, which could mean either "hollow," or "grassy hill."

CIAN m. (key-in) "ancient, enduring." This name occurs in legend, and was also borne by the son-in-law of Brian Boru, Cian Mac Mael Muad (mac mail moo-ad) who led the armies from the south to victory over the Vikings at the Battle of Clontarf. In the past, the name was Anglicized as Kean, Keane, King, and even Cain, but presently it is being revived in Ireland in its old form.

CIANNAIT f. (keya-nit) This is a feminine form of Cian, meaning "ancient" or "enduring." It might be Anglicized Keenat or Kinnat.

CLIONA/Clíodhna f. (klee-ona) A name that occurs in legend, usually that of a fairy woman. As Clídna, she appears as one of the mythical race, the Tuatha Dé Danann (two-a-ha day dan-an). Another Cliona was a fairy patroness of the MacCarthys. Well-used today in Ireland, it also occurs as Cleona.

CLODAGH f. (klo-da) From Clóideach, the name of a river in County Waterford. Cloda is also used.

CLOONEY/Cluny m. A name possibly derived from *cluain,* "grassy meadow." More usually encountered as a surname but ripe for use as a first name in the coming millennium, for a girl or a boy.

CODY m. A name originating from the surname Mac Óda, "son of Otto," Otto being an old German name signifying prosperity. Formerly very popular in the United States as a boy's name, possibly with reference to the historical figure of Buffalo Bill Cody, it is currently finding favor as a girl's name. Kody, Codi, Kodie, and Kodee are various forms.

COLE/Comhghall/Comgall m. The name has been interpreted as "co-pledge" and as "fellow hostage." Pledges were people, often children, exchanged between warring families as assurance to keep peace. Some ten saints were said to have carried the name, the most famous of whom was abbot of Bangor, County Down. Cowal is an alternative Anglicized form.

COLL/Colla m. An early name with a meaning like "great chief, high lord." The name was used by three distinguished-warrior brothers who were claimed as ancestors by families in the north and west. It survived down to the late nineteenth century.

COLLEEN/Colene/Collene f. The name derives from the Irish *cailín,* meaning "a girl." It was first used by emigrant families who settled in the United States, Australia, and South Africa, as a way of maintaining and declaring national roots. It is rarely encountered in Ireland, but is still in evidence in other English-speaking countries.

COMGAN/Comghán m. (ko-an or ko-gan) Some have interpreted this name to mean "co-birth," hence "twin." Saint Comgan was an eighth-century chieftain of Leinster exiled to Scotland where he eventually founded a monastery and several churches. Cowan and Coan are Anglicized forms.

CONLETH/Connlaodh m. "great lord, great chief," with a similar root as Coll. Despite such origins, the name was well used by clergy of record up until the seventeenth century. Connla, Condla, and Conle are other forms.

COREY m. In Ireland, this name is thought to have derived from a variety of surnames that include the root *corra,* "spear." Though rarely used as a first name there, it became popular in the United States as a boy's name, especially in the 1960s. Corie, Cory, Corry, and Korey are variable spell-

ings, with Cori, Korri, and Correye being used as feminine
forms.

DÁIBHÍ m. (daw-vee) This is the Irish form of Davey, the
pet form of David, a biblical name meaning "beloved,
friend." It was and is more widely used than Daibhead (daw-
vade), which is the translation of David.

DÁIRE m. (daw-re) This is the name of an old divinity
meaning "fruitful one." The name occurs frequently in legend. One saint who bore the name was a woman, and from
time to time, as with other early names, it may have been
used by both sexes.

DALEY/DALY m. From the Irish Dálach, meaning "frequenter of gatherings." It shares the same root as the word
for the Irish parliament, the Dáil. The surname O'Daly derives from this name.

DANA f. (dan-ah) In Ireland, this is a very old name deriving
from a Celtic goddess also known as Anu and Danu. As a
river goddess, there are many European rivers that took her
name; the Danube and the Don are examples. In Ireland, she
was identified as a mother goddess, and the mythical race of
beings said to have first inhabited the lands, the Tuatha Dé
Danann ("people of Dana") were named for her. The popular use of the name in this century, for men and women,
may more likely be attributed to the German-originated surname which means "a Dane."

DARBY m. This name is an English import that took root
originally as a translation for Dermot or Diarmaid.

DECLAN m. It has been suggested that this name originates from the elements *deagh,* "good," and *lan,* "full." The Gaelic form is Deaglán. The earliest-known carrier was Saint Declan of Ardmore, thought to have been one of the earliest Christian missionaries in Ireland and a precursor of Saint Patrick. The name has been well-used in Ireland and is beginning to find favor in other countries.

DEIRDRE f. (deer-dre) The meaning for this name is not certain, but it may derive from a very early name meaning "she who chatters." Deirdre is a tragic heroine in Irish mythology. The most beautiful woman of her time, she caught the eye of King Conor Mac Nessa, who demanded her hand in marriage. Deirdre loved the young warrior Naoise and eloped with him to Scotland. Conor sent word to them of his forgiveness and bade them return but treacherously murdered Naoise when the couple came back to Ireland. Deirdre, rather than live without her beloved, threw herself from a chariot, ending her own life. Her story was celebrated by twentieth-century writers W. B. Yeats and John Millington Synge. The name has been popular in English-speaking countries since the 1920s. The old Irish form is written Derdriu, but subsequent forms have produced Deidre, Deidra, Diedra, and Derdre.

DERMOT/Dermott m. The Irish form of this name is Diarmaid or Diarmait, and it has loosely been translated to mean "envy-free." A popular early name, it has been used consistently in Ireland. In legend, Diarmait Ua Duibne (dee-ermit ooa dib-na) was the greatest lover in Ireland, and he provoked the wrath of Finn Mac Cool by eloping with Grania, Finn's betrothed. For sixteen years, Diarmait and Grania lived as fugitives, eluding Finn and his men, but were finally overtaken and tragedy ensued. Diarmuid and Diarmid

are alternative forms, and the name has been translated to
Jerome, Jeremiah, Darby, Derby, and Derry.

DERVLA f. (der-vla) This is the contemporary Anglicized
form used for two older names, one written Dearbhail (der-
voll) meaning "daughter of Fal," Fal being a name for Ireland in legend, and the other Deirbhile (der-vila) meaning
"daughter of a poet." Princesses and saints of record have
borne both names. Derval is another form, and more recently,
the new Irish spellings Dearbhla and Dearbhaile have been
used.

DERVORGILLA f. (der-vor-gilla) From the older Irish
Dearbhorgaill, "daughter of Forgall," Forgall being a god.
The name occurs in legend as that of an admirer of Cúchulainn and as that of a queen who left her husband for the
king of a neighboring province and later established a church
at Clonmacnoise.

DESMOND m. This name has been well-used in the
English-speaking world for some time. It comes from the old
source Desmumhnach (das-u-nach), "man from Desmond."
Desmond was a province in the south and derives from Deas
Mumhan, meaning "south Munster." This territory, located
in County Cork, was home to several powerful dynasties, the
first being the MacCarthys, then later the Norman settlers,
the FitzGeralds. Deasún is a later Irish translation back from
the Anglo form Desmond.

DONAL/Donall m. (doe-nil) This name enjoyed great popularity from early times. In the Gaelic form, it is Domhnall,
domhan meaning "world," and is interpreted to mean
"world-mighty." It has been used by numerous kings
through the ages, and in the eleventh century, there are rec-

ords of two regents, both with the name Donal, who engaged in a duel to the death. By the seventeenth century, the name was so prevalent, it was used as a term for a Catholic Irishman. In Scotland, the name was equally well-used and took the form Donald. There are three saints who bore the name. It was Anglicized as Daniel, and Donie is a pet form.

DONEGAL m. (dun-e-gaul) This is a name borrowed from the place name that derives from Dún na nGall (doon na ngall), meaning "fort of the foreigners," referring to the Viking stronghold of the tenth century.

DWYER m. (d'-wire) This is an Anglicized form of the Irish surname O Duibhidir (o dweer), which is composed of elements *dubh,* "black, dark," and *eidir,* "sense, wisdom."

EALGA f. (al-ga) "noble." A rarely used name that derives from a poetic name for Ireland, Innis Ealga, which means "noble isle."

ÉAMONN/Éamon/Éamann m. (ay-man) This is the Irish form of Edmund, a name introduced by the Normans meaning "rich protection." It proved popular then and is widely used today, possibly with reference to the political figure of Éamon de Valera, president of Ireland from 1959 to 1973, and a central figure in the emergence of the Republic of Ireland.

ÉIBHEAR m. (ay-ver) Éibhear was one of the mythical figures who led the Gaels to Ireland. His name appears to derive from Eberus, which is itself an Irish form of the Latin Hibernus, meaning "Irishman." The name was well-used in the nineteenth century. In English, it was rendered as Harry,

Ivor, and Heber. A more contemporary and suitable Anglicization might be Ever.

EILEEN/Eibhlín f. (i-leen) This is an Irish form of Aveline
or Avelina, a name introduced by the conquering Normans.
In England, it became Evelyn or Evelina. Its meaning is not
clear but might be something like "wished-for child." Aibhílín is another Irish form the name took, which gave rise to
the currently popular name Aileen. In the past, the name was
Anglicized as Helen, Ellen, Ella, and Ellie. Eileen was well-
used in the English-speaking world in the early part of this
century but has recently been superseded by Aileen. Ilene is
a common spelling found in the United States.

EILIS f. (i-lish) This is an Irish form of the biblical name
Elizabeth, "God is my oath." Popular in medieval times, it
is still quietly used in Ireland. Eilish, Eillish, and Eibhlís are
alternative forms.

ÉIRE f. (air-ih) Éire was one of a triad of goddesses who
vied to have the land of Ireland named after her. She was
victorious over her sisters Banbha and Fodhla. Her name was
used as a first name in early times but is rarely found today.
The more popularly used Erin derives from this name.

EIREEN f. (air-een) This contemporary name is thought to
derive from a combination of Éire with the Irish diminutive
element -een, or from an Irish elaboration of the name Irene,
"peace."

EIRNÍN f. & m. (air-neen) Probably a name that comes from
the word *iarn,* "iron." There are sixteen saints of record,
both male and female, who bore the name. Earnan (er-nawn)
is a related masculine form, and Ernan an Anglicized form.

EMER/Eimear/Eimer/Emir f. (ee-mer) Emer was the wife of Cúchulainn. Despite her father, Forgall's objection to the match, Cúchulainn single-handedly stormed Forgall's fortress and carried Emer off. Cúchulainn was not a faithful husband, but Emer endured his philandering stoically until he made love to Fand, wife of the sea god Manannán. When she confronted the lovers, she realized the strength of Fand's love and offered to withdraw. Touched by this display of unselfishness, Fand elected to return to her husband. Upon his death, Emer went on to speak movingly and lovingly at her husband's graveside. The name has been well-used in Ireland in the twentieth century and occurs in Scotland as Eamhair and Éimhear pronounced "ayv-er."

EMMET m. (em-et) The popular use of this surname as a first name is with connection to the patriot Robert Emmet, who led the unsuccessful rebellion of the United Irishmen against the British in 1798. Emmet gave a moving speech at the scene of his execution in Dublin in 1803, which begins, "Let no one write my epitaph . . ." The surname Emmet derives from the Germanic feminine name Emma, "all-embracing."

EOIN m. (owen) Eoin is an Irish form of the biblical name John, "God is gracious," which comes from the Latin form, Iohannes. It is a distinct name from the earlier Irish Eoghan, pronounced similarly. Understandably, the two have been confused at times, both being Anglicized as Owen.

ERIN f. (ear-in) A name that may be interpreted to mean "of Éire," Éire being the ordinary Irish name for Ireland. A name that was popularly adopted by Irish immigrants in Australia, Canada, and the United States. Forms that have evolved are Erinn, Eryn, Erina, and Aryn.

EVIN m. From the Irish name Éimhín (ayv-een), "swift, ready." Monasterevan is named for its patron and founder, Saint Éimhín. Evan is another possible Anglicization, though both forms are commonly thought of as Welsh, where they are used as a form of John.

FÁINNE f. (fawn-ye) An Irish word for "ring," which is beginning to find use as a first name.

FALLON f. & m. From the Irish names Faithleann or Fallamhan, meaning "leader." Usually encountered as a surname, it has recently been adopted as a first name useful for girls or boys.

FAOILEANN f. (fee-lan) A name interpreted as "a graceful woman." Two princesses of record and two saints have borne the name.

FARQUHAR m. (fark-uhar) A name that comes from the Irish Fearchar, made from the elements *fear*, "man," and *cara*, "friend." This spelling is more usually found, as a first and surname, in Scotland.

FARRELL m. This is an Anglicization of the name Fergal. In Ireland today, it is more usually encountered as a surname. Recently, however, in the United States it is being used, along with Farall, as a first name.

FARRY m. This is the Anglicized form of the early name Fearadhach (far-ay-ach), which means "manly." The name occurs in early writings and was used by kings in Ireland and Scotland.

FEARGANAINM m. (far-gan-anm) "man without a name" is the literal translation of this name, which was used quite frequently in the early modern period. Most likely it alludes to the notion of individual independence. It was Anglicized as Ferdinand.

FEME f. (fe-va) "young woman, a girl." This name was borne by a virgin saint of the O'Neill family. The old Gaelic spelling probably begs a contemporary formulation.

FERDIA m. (fer-dia) In fable, Ferdia was the good friend of the Ulster hero Cúchulainn. Maeve, queen of Connacht, commanded Ferdia to challenge his friend who was the lone sentry at a strategically located ford between the provinces of Connacht and Ulster. The duel lasted for over three days, and it was only by the use of magic that Cúchulainn finally overcame Ferdia. The name is in current use in Ireland.

FERGUS/Fearghus m. "man strength" or "man vigor" is a translation for this name. It was very popularly used from an early period, and many kings of record owned the name. In fable, Fergus Mac Erc, with his two brothers, led his tribe, the Scots, across the sea to the northern part of Britain, founding the kingdom of Argyl, "the eastern Gael," in the land that has come to be known as Scotland. Understandably, the name is widely used in Scotland and is also still common in Ireland.

FIDELMA f. (fe-delm-a) This is the most commonly used form of the early Irish name Fedelm. Many famous women bore the name in early times, including a daughter of the Ulster king, Conor Mac Nessa, who was known as Fedelm Noíchrothach (nee-cro-hach), "the nine-times beautiful," a warrior of some note herself. Six saints of record used the name. It has been suggested that it derives from *feidhle,* meaning "constancy." Fedelma is another spelling.

FINEEN/Fínín m. (fin-een) "wine-birth." This was a popular name in early times, used by kings and warriors. One Fineen was physician to King Conor Mac Nessa. Finneen, Finnin, Fingin, and Finghin are other forms. The name was translated as Florence from as early as the thirteenth century, and Florence has been used as a male name in Ireland since, along with shortened forms Florry, Florrie, Flurry, and Flur.

FÍRINNE f. (feer-inna) "truth, fidelity," a name with the same meaning as Verity.

FÍTHEAL m. (fee-hal) "a sprite, goblin." An early Irish name associated with a judge of unshakable authority. In legend, Finn Mac Cool's brother was said to be called Fítheal. It was Anglicized as Florence or Florry.

FLAHERTY m. From the old Irish Flaithbheartach (fla-hartach) meaning "princely, lordly in action." This was a name borne by many kings, especially in Connacht, where the dynasty of the O'Flahertys was based. More usually found as a surname today in Ireland.

FLAITHEAS f. (flaw-his) With a meaning like "sovereignty." Flaitheas was a fairy woman patroness of the O'Neill family.

FODHLA/Fodla f. (foe-la) Fodhla was one of the Otherworldly beings, the Tuatha Dé Danann. Described as "one of their shapely women," she was sister to Banbha and Éire, and with them, her name is sometimes used as a poetic name for Ireland.

FROSSACH/Frassach m. (frus-ach) Possibly from *frass,* "shower." Frassach was the name of an early Irish saint and hermit.

FUAMNACH f. (foo-am-nach) In legend, Fuamnach was the wife of Midhir. When she detected an amorous alliance between her husband and the beautiful Etain, she changed Etain into a scarlet fly.

GAEL m. (gale) Popular legend holds that Gael was the original ancestor from whom the Gaelic peoples descended. To a modern ear, the name is equally suitable as a girl's name.

GALLAGHER m. (gal-a-her) The surname used as a first name. It originates from the name Gallchobhar (gaul-chor), meaning "lover of foreigners."

GALWAY m. This is a borrowing of the place name as a first name. The town of Galway takes its name from *gall,* meaning "stone." *Gall* is also the Irish word to indicate a foreigner.

GARVAN m. From the Irish name Garbhán, which stems from the root *garbh* (gorv), "rough." The name was borne by an early king of Munster, as well as five saints. Garvin is an alternative spelling.

GILLESPIE m. From the Irish, Giolla Easpaig (gyulla as-pig). *Giolla* was a well-used element in early naming meaning "servant" or "devotee"; *easpaig* is "bishop," hence "devotee of the bishop." Giolla was shortened to Gil- in time, and many contemporary surnames show the form: Gilpatrick, Gilbride, Gilchrist, Gilmore, Gilroy, and so on.

GILLIGAN m. From Gillagán (gul-agawn), with a meaning like "little lad." An early name that occurs usually as a surname today.

GLENN/Glen m. Contemporary use as a first name of the Irish word *gleann* (glown), meaning "valley." The Welsh form, Glyn, has been in use for some time.

GOBÁN/Gobbán m. (gub-awn) Goibniu (gub-na) was the ancient god of craftsmanship, and *goba* (guba) is the old Irish for "smith," as in goldsmith. Gobán derives from either of these two sources. Gobán Saor (sayre) was the master craftsman of Irish folk legend. Several saints of record bore the name.

GOBNET/Gobnait f. (gub-nit) This name, somewhat charmless to contemporary sensibilites, was widely used in Ireland during the early and Middle Ages. It is probably a feminine form of Gobán, but some have attributed it the separate origin of deriving from *gob,* meaning "mouth" or "beak." Saint Gobnet of Ballyvourney in County Cork is the most famous saint to have borne the name. She was foundress of several monasteries and credited with the working of several miracles. She is known as the patron saint of beekeepers. Perhaps this explains why the name was translated as Deborah, a Hebraic name meaning "bee," as well as Abigail, Abbie, and Debbie. Gobnat, Gubnet, and Gobinet are alternative forms, and it was sometimes shortened to Gubby and Webby.

GOFRAIDH/Gofraí m. (guf-ry) This is the Irish form of the Germanic name Godafrid, better known as Godfrey, meaning "god's peace." The name was introduced by the Vikings and was well used in the Middle Ages, especially in the north. In the nineteenth century, one Gofraidh Mac Cion-naith (mac keenath) left a deathbed curse on any of his race that would revive the name after his passing.

GUAIRE m. (gware-eh) "noble, proud." A relatively common early name, with records of kings and saints as bearers.

GUS m. A very early Irish name with the meaning "force, vigor." It died out in usage as an individual name, but occurs as an element in names such as Fergus and Aengus.

HONOR f. This name came to Ireland with the Anglo-Normans, originally as Honora, from the Latin term for "honor." It proved popular and was rendered in Irish Onóra. From it originate the popular Irish forms of Norah, Noreen, and Nonie, as well as use of the names Hanorah, Noirín, Nora, Noinín, Nanno, and Daisy.

INA f. (eena) Some have suggested this name to be an Irish form of Agnes, which occurs also as Aigneis. Its continued use may more likely be as a pet form of any name ending -ina.

IRIAL m. (ir-ee-al) An old Irish name with obscure origins and meaning. Revived in the Middle Ages by several families. A name that has the ring of a contemporary appeal about it.

ISEULT f. (is-ult) This name occurs in Arthurian legend as that of an Irish princess who was betrothed to the elderly King Mark of Cornwall. To ensure her happiness, Iseult's mother prepared a love potion for her daughter so that she might find the match agreeable. Unfortunately, by mistake, Iseult shared the potion with Mark's young nephew, Tristan, and the two were doomed to lasting adulterous love. Yseult, Isolde, and Isolda are alternative forms.

ITA/Ida f. (ee-ta or ee-da) From the Irish Íte. This name is interpreted to mean "thirst," but literal translation proffers the meaning as "the act of eating, devouring." The name was widely used in reverence to Saint Ita, a prominent sixth-century saint who chose the name herself as an allusion to her hunger for divine love. She was known as "the foster mother of the saints," and she founded a famous monastery in Limerick known as Kileedy (Ida's church).

JARLATH m. (jar-lath) This name comes from the Irish Iarflaith, or Iarlaith, which some have interpreted to mean "tributary lord." Saint Jarlath was a sixth-century bishop of Tuam in County Galway, where he established an important monastery and school. The name also occurs as Hierlaith.

KEELY f. This is a contemporary form that may have been drawn from Caoilfhionn/Keelin, or it may be read as a feminine form of the male name Kiely. The root of all these names is *cadhla,* "beautiful, graceful." Their phonetic sound is proving especially popular at the moment. Keeley, Keelie, Keily, and Kiely are alternative spellings.

KEENAN m. From Cianán, a diminutive form of Cian, "ancient one." More usually found as a surname today in Ireland, the name is currently achieving a measure of popularity in the United States. Keenen, Keenon, Kienan, and Kenan are variable forms.

KERMIT m. This name arises from the Irish surname MacDermot. It is likely too closely associated with the famous green frog from the television series *The Muppets* to be easily used any time soon in the English-speaking world. Another form however, Kermode, presents a possibility.

KEVIN m. From Caoimhín (kwee-veen), which means "beautiful birth" or "comely child." Kevin was a seventh-century saint, famous for his piety and patience. He established a famous monastery at Glendalough, County Wicklow, which became an important site of pilgrimage. The name has been used very widely around the world since the early part of the century, specifically in Britain and the United States. In 1994, it was cited as the most popularly chosen boy's name in France. Very recently, however, there has been a sharp decline in its usage in Britain and the United States. The spelling Keven is sometimes used, and Kevina (kev-eena) is a feminine form.

LASSARINA f. (loss-arena) From the Irish, Lasairíona, from a compound of *lasair* "flame," and *fion* "wine," with an interpretation like "fire of wine." It was a popular name in the later Middle Ages, especially in the west. Lasrina is a shortened form.

LEABHARCHAM f. (lowr-cham) "slender, stooped." In legend, Leabharcham is the faithful nurse of Deirdre. Another Leabharcham was one of Cúchulainn's lovers.

LEARBHEAN f. (lar-van) "lady of the sea." This name was borne by an eighth-century abbess in Roscommon, known as Learbhan Bán (bawn), "the white."

LEARY m. From the Irish Laoghaire or Laoire (leer-a). The meaning is "calf-herd." It was an early name used by several prominent figures, one king of record, and two saints. The surname O'Leary derives from it.

LENNAN m. From the Irish Leannán (lan-awn), meaning "sweetheart, lover." The surnames O'Linnane, Leonard, and Lennon all stem from this name.

LIA f. (lee-ah) Contemporary use of the word for "gray" as a feminine name, echoing the well-used forms Leah and Lea of separate origins.

LIADAN f. (lia-din) "gray lady." Liadan was a poet beloved by Cuirithir (quir-ihir), himself a poet. By the time he met her, she had become a nun. Cuirithir became a monk, and they lived out their love without breaking their vows of chastity. There is also a saint of the name who is claimed as a patron by the Dál Cais (dall cosh), "people of Cas."

LIADHNÁN m. (lee-an-awn) "gray lad." Two saints of record have carried this name. Leanan is a possible Anglicization.

LIAM m. This is the more popular Irish form of the Germanic name William, a compound name meaning "will helmet." Uilliam is the older more formal Irish translation, but Liam is much more widely used, currently gaining popularity in the United States and recently figuring in the top ten selected names for boys in Britain.

LIAMHAIN f. (lia-vin) This name has a meaning like "comely." In popular tradition, Liamhain is sister to Saint Patrick.

LIBAN f. (lee-ban) From the Irish Lí Bhan (lee vawn), with a meaning like "beauty of women." Liban was a mythical lady, known also as Muirgein (mwir-gin), who lived beneath the waters of Lough Neagh for three hundred years. She was eventually caught by a fisherman and baptized into the Christian church.

LIFE f. (lif-ee) Folk legend tells of a lady of this name for whom the river Liffey, which flows through Dublin, was named. It is likely, however, that the river's name is older than this tale. James Joyce celebrated the river and its mythical personification in the figure of Anna Livia Plurabelle of *Finnegan's Wake*.

LOCHLANN m. (loch-lan) This was a name signifying a Viking in the past, Norway being known as the "land of the lochs." As the Vikings settled and intermarried with the Irish, the name began to be used freely and was a popular first name. It was Anglicized as Laughlin and Loughlin, and Lockie and Lachie are pet forms.

LOMAN m. (low-man) From Irish Lomán (lom-awn), meaning "bare." Several saints bore the name, one of them said to have been a nephew of Saint Patrick.

LORETTA f. This is a borrowing of the place name, Loreto, in Italy, a center of pilgrimage that was supposed to hold the house of the Virgin Mary, allegedly transported there from Nazareth by angels. The Irish order of the Sisters of Loretto trained Mother Teresa of Calcutta. The name has been attractive in the past to devout Irish Catholics.

MAEVE/Meadhbh/Maebh/Madhbh f. (mayv) "intoxicating, she who makes men drunk." This is an early name, originally that of a goddess. In the earliest times, it was used by both men and women, but since has been exclusively used for women. The most famous bearer is probably Maeve, Queen of Connacht, the headstrong regent who features in

the tale "Taín Bó Cuailgne" (tawn bo quilye), "the cattle
raid of Cooley," and who eventually caused the death of
Cúchulainn in her war on Ulster. The name has been popularly used since medieval times, had a fashionable resurgence
in the thirties and forties, and is currently once again well in
favor. Medbh, Meibh, Mave, and Mab are various forms
found, as well as the diminutives Meaveen, Meidhbhín, and
Mabbina.

MÁIRE f. (moy-ra) This is an Irish form of the name Mary.
Although we think of Mary as a typical Irish name, it was
rarely used, in reverence of the figure of the Virgin Mary,
as a first name until the beginning of the seventeenth century.
This pattern reflected similar usage in other European countries. Instead, connected forms such as Gilla Muire (gilla
mwira), "servant of Mary," and Maol Muire (mwale
mwira), "devotee of Mary," were used. The huge popularity
of the name begins only in modern times and probably owes
much to the translation of Mór, a very popular existent name,
as Mary. In the early decades of the twentieth century, Mary
and its various forms had overwhelmed all competition, with
a reckoning as high as one in every four Irish women bearing
some form of the name. As well as Máire, the multitude of
forms that developed in Ireland includes Maille, Mailse,
Mailti, Mallaidh, Máirín, and some Anglicized equivalents,
Moira, Moyra, Maura, Maureen, May, Molly, Moll, and Ma-
mie. Continental forms Maria and Marie (pronounced mahr-
ee, with the stress on the first syllable) are also well used in
Ireland.

MAIREAD/Mairéad f. (maw-raid) The Irish form of Margaret. This name became very popular once it came into fashion about the fourteenth century, and many forms have
ensued. Maighread, Mairghréad, Maraid, Muirghead, and

Máirgrég are some, and the English pet forms Meg and Peggy were rendered as Meigín, Peig, Peigí, Peigín, and Pegeen.

MAITIÚ m. (mot-yoo) The Irish form of the biblical Matthew, "gift of God."

MAJELLA f. This is a borrowing of the surname of the eighteenth-century saint, Gerard Majella. Gerard is the patron saint of mothers and childbirth, and his first name also is popularly used in Ireland.

MALACHY m. (mal-a-kee) This name derives from the earlier Irish name Mael Sechlainn (mail ech-lin), "devotee of Saint Sechnall." High kings in the ninth and tenth centuries bore the name. In the late Middle Ages, it became very popular, possibly with allusion to the biblical name Malachi, meaning "my messenger."

MALONE m. The Irish surname used for a first name. It comes from the Irish form Maol Eoin, "servant of (Saint) John." Unusual as a first name in Ireland.

MANNIX m. An Anglicization of the earlier pet names Mainchín and Munchin, "little monk." Not surprisingly several saints have borne the name, and at least one television detective.

MANUS m. This is an Irish form of the Latin Magnus, "great." Its popularity throughout Europe stems from the figure of Charlemagne, or Carolus Magnus in Latin. Brought to Ireland by the Vikings, it began to be used frequently around the twelfth century, especially in the north. Maghnus (mawn-us) is another form.

MAOLÍOSA f. & m. (mwail-ee-sa) "devotee of Jesus." At first a name used by clerics, as early as the tenth century the name became popular with the laity. For the most part, it was a male name, but now is being used for girls, perhaps due to a resemblance to, and as a distinctly Irish twist on, the popular Melissa.

MAON f. & m. (mane) An old name, originally borne by a god, meaning "silent." In early folklore it is more frequently found as a female name. Conn of the Hundred Battles had a daughter called Maon.

MAONACH m. (mane-och) Deriving from Maon, "silent." This was the more popular form used by men. Several distinguished churchmen bore the name. From it we get the contemporary surname O'Mooney or Mooney.

MARGA f. (mor-ga) An old name from folklore sources, with no obvious meaning. Marga of the fairy mound was mother of the unfortunate Etain.

MARMADUKE m. This rather Anglo-sounding name derives from the Irish Mael Madoc (mail may-ogue), "devotee of (Saint) Madoc." The best-known carrier of the name, Saint Mael Madoc O Morgair of the twelfth century, is better known as Saint Malachy of Armagh, the influential church reformer. The name was frequently rendered as Malachy. It is thought that the area of Marmaduke in north England is called after this name due to its adoption by the Viking settlers who were eventually ousted from Dublin.

MAUREEN f. This is a pet form of Máire, but one that has taken on a life of its own. It could easily be linked with a pet form of the old name Mór, Moreen, but is really separate in origin. Widely used in the twentieth century throughout the English-speaking world, Máirín, Maurene, Maurine, and Moirean are varied forms, Mo, Moe, and Maury being pet forms.

MEAGHER m. (ma-her) Usually found as a surname, this name derives from an older Irish form, Meachar, meaning "fine, majestic." It is commonly associated with the south, and there is an early saint of the name.

MIACH f. & m. (mee-ach) An old name from legend. Miach was one of the Tuatha Dé Danann, the son of Diancecht, a preeminent craftsman. When the king, Nuada, lost his hand in battle, Diancecht made a replacement out of silver. Miach went one better and fashioned a hand from flesh and bone. The name means "honorable, proud," and it was used by women also.

MICHEÁL m. (me-haul) The Irish form of the biblical name Michael, "Who is like the Lord?" Well-used in the last century in Irish and English forms, eventually becoming associated with the idea of an Irishman, especially in the shortened form, Mick. Mike, Mikey, and Mickey are also commonly used forms.

MILO m. This name derives from the names Myles and Miles in Ireland. The names Maeleachlainn, Maolmhuire, and Maolmordha, all beginning with the element *mael*, "devotee of ———," were translated as Myles and Miles. Milo, in turn, is an Irish spin on these names.

MOCHTA m. (much-ta) Early name with a probable meaning of "great."

MOLLY f. This is essentially a pet form of Máire. It was widely used from the eighteenth century on, and not just in Ireland. By the nineteenth century, it had earned a rather seedy reputation and fell from favor. In the 1930s, it began to reappear and proved popular once again, but the wave was short-lived. Currently, it is being revived to a great degree along with other "unpretentious" names with a period feel. Strong Irish associations occur in the figure of Molly Malone, who features in the well-known song, "Cockles and Mussels," and with the nineteenth-century secret society, the Molly Maguires.

MONA f. In Ireland, the use of Mona stems from the Irish name Muadhnait (mu-anat) meaning "noble, good." Monat was another Anglicized form of Muadhnait, but Mona is the form usually encountered today, and it is echoed in the use of the name as either a shortened form of Monica, a use of the Arabic name, or reference to the Italian *madonna*.

MOR/Mór f. (more) "tall, great." This was by far the most popularly used name for women for a long period during the medieval times. Several queens of record bore the name, and it was used by ruling families well into the sixteenth century. The name was translated variously as Martha and Agnes, but most frequently as Mary, the name that eventually replaced it. Well-used in Scotland also, it gave rise there to the popular diminutive, Morag. In Ireland, the pet forms were Moirin and Moreen, which were not surprisingly confused with the name Maureen.

MUGHAIN f. (moon) An old name from the south born by a goddess. The meaning is thought to be "a young maiden." Two saints bore the name.

MUIRIOS/Muirgius m. (mwir-i-osh) An old name meaning "sea strength." It was well-used by royal lineages in the west and persisted through to late medieval times. It was translated as Maurice and eventually retranslated as Muiris.

MUIRIS m. (mwir-ish) This is the Irish form of Maurice, a name introduced by the Normans, originally from the Latin Mauritius, "Moorish, dark-skinned." It was popularly used in Ireland in reverence to the martyr Saint Maurice. Distinctive Irish pet forms include Moss and Mossy.

MURRY m. From the old Irish Muiríoch (mwir-ee-och) or Muireadhach (mwir-ahach), with possible translations "a lord, a master" or "seaman." A name with strong regal associations in the west. Ten members of the legendary royal bodyguard, the Fianna (fee-ana), bore the name. It is well-used in Scotland and is Anglicized as Murray, a common surname there.

MURTAGH m. (murt-a) This is the Anglicized form of an early name, Muircheartach (mwir-khart-ah), "skilled in seacraft, mariner." It was a very common name in the early and medieval periods, borne by several kings of record, two in the twelfth century. Through its history of usage, it acquired numerous forms: Mreartach, Moriartach, and Briartach, and several translations: Mortimer, Murt, Murty, Monty, and Maurice. Usually encountered today as a surname, Murtaugh is another contemporary spelling.

MYRNA f. From the Irish Muirne (mwir-na), "high-spirited, festive." Muirne was mother of the mythical champion Finn Mac Cool.

NAOISE m. (nee-sha) A name without clear origins, though it may contain the element *nasc*, "bond." In legend, Naoise was the beloved of Deirdre and was treacherously murdered, with his brothers, by King Conchobhar Mac Nessa (kru-hoor), the man from whom he had won her. The name was translated as Noah, and Nyce is an Anglo form.

NÁPLA f. (naw-pla) An Irish form of Annabelle, a name introduced by the Normans. The earlier Irish form was Annábla (an-aw-bla), but this shortened form replaced it.

NEACHT f. (ny-acht) Rare early name meaning "pure."

NEILA f. This is a contemporary feminine form of Niall. Nelda, Neala, and Nilda are also used.

NESSA/Neasa f. (nes-sa or ny-assa) Nessa was the legendary mother of Conchobhar Mac Nessa. Originally, her name was Assa (ossa), meaning "gentle," but when she was compelled to take up arms against her husband Cathbad, she did so with such success that she became known as Ní Assa (nee ossa), "not gentle." A shrewd and ambitious woman, she artfully brought her son to the throne by cutting a deal with her brother-in-law, Fergus. Nessa was also the name of a sister to Saint Ita.

NEVAN m. From the Irish Naomhán (nave-awn), which derives from *naomh* (nave), "saint, holy one." Originally a nickname for a churchman, it became used as a first name and later a surname. Nevin, Neven, and Niven are related forms.

NOLAN m. Use of the Irish surname as a first name. Nolan possibly derives from the word nuall, "shout" or "noble."

Usually found in the United States, Nolen is another spelling, and Noland an elaboration.

NOLLAIG f. & m. (nul-ig) This is the Irish word for Christmas, from the French form Noel. Used only in modern times as a first name, it is more usually encountered in the common forms Noel and Noelle.

NUADHA m. (nu-a) This is an early name associated with a god, possibly of the Otherworld, possibly of fishermen. It is interpreted to mean "the cloud-maker." Heroes, saints, and clerics have borne the name.

OILIBHÉAR m. (oliver) This is an Irish form of Oliver, a name introduced via Britain by the Normans. The name originates perhaps from the Norse name Olaf, "heir to his ancestors," or from a French adaptation of the feminine Olive, a name taken from the tree. Popular for a while, it was widely avoided after the punitive atrocities inflicted by Oliver Cromwell in the seventeenth century. In the twentieth century, it has found new favor, used with reverence to the figure of Saint Oliver Plunket, a martyred bishop canonized as recently as 1976.

OISTÍN m. (ish-teen) An Irish form of the Norse name Austin, itself a form of Augustine, from the Latin *venerable*. Records reveal usage as early as the ninth century.

PARTHALAN/Parthalon/Parthalán m. (parth-a-lon) This is an Irish translation of the biblical Bartholomew, "son of Talmai." In folk legend, Parthalan was the first leader to settle in Ireland after the the biblical flood of the Old Testament. Párthlán (parth-lawn), Partnán (part-nawn), and

Beartlaidh (bartley) are variant forms, and it was Anglicized
as Berkley, Barclay, Bartley, and Batt.

PATRICIA f. The feminine form of Patrick, Ireland's patron
saint. Patricia has only been commonly used in Ireland in
the twentieth century, probably occurring more widely in
other countries initially. Records of a seventh-century Italian
saint, Patricia of Naples, exist. The name originates from the
Latin *patricius,* "a noble, an aristocrat." Pádraigín, the Irish
form used, was earlier employed as a diminutive for the male
name Pádraig. The familiar shortened form, Patsy, is often
still used for men in Ireland, but Pat, Patty, Paddy, and Paití
are commonly found.

PATRICK m. From the Latin, *patricius,* "noble." Saint Patrick is internationally known and celebrated as Ireland's patron saint. He was, in fact, British, kidnapped as a boy and
held as a slave for six years in Ireland. He eventually escaped
and trained as a priest, probably in France. His ambition was
to return as a missionary to Ireland and convert the natives
to Christianity. All evidence suggests that he had great success with this plan, and by his death in 463, much of the
country had abandoned older pagan ways. He was held in
such great esteem thoughout Ireland that Patrick, or the Irish
form Pádraig (paw-rig), was not used as a first name by the
native Irish until about the seventeenth century. In the nineteenth century, it became so prevalent that it was considered
a generic name for an Irish man. Typically, forms abounded:
Pádhraic, Páraic, Pádhraig, Padhrig, Phaedrig (faw-drig), and
Paidraic, with pet forms Páid (pawdge), Páidi (paw-jee), Pái-
dín (paw-jeen), Páiti (paw-chee), Parra, Padhra (para), Pau-
deen, Pat, Paddy, Pad, and Pa. The name has been well used
internationally in this century—in France it has come to rival
the native French form, Patrice—with periodic fluxes in use

and disuse according to fashion. In Ireland, the form Pádraig experienced a resurgence in the last decade, though Patrick is now back and well-established in the Irish top ten.

PEADAR/Peadair m. (pa-ther) This is an Irish form of Peter, from *petrus,* ''rock.'' Peadar is a later evolution, Peter previously having been rendered as Piaras, from the Norman-introduced name, Piers. Peadar has been well-used in Ireland this century.

PHELIM/Felim m. (fay-lim) From the Irish Feidhlim or Feidhlimid (fay-lim-ee). An old name of uncertain meaning, possibly connected with the word *feidhil,* ''constant, always.'' The name occurs in legend and in early royal records; three kings of Munster bore it. Popularly used since the early period and up to the later Middle Ages, when it was also sparingly used as a girl's name, it is still found in Ireland today.

PHILOMENA f. This is a borrowing of the Latin name interpreted as ''beloved.'' At the beginning of the nineteenth century, the cult of a Saint Philomena of Rome flourished and resulted in a popular adoption of the name in Ireland by Roman Catholics. The Vatican officially suppressed her cult in 1960, and subsequent use has declined sharply.

PIARAS m. (peer-ash) The Irish form of Piers, itself an old Norman form of Peter. Feoras (fee-orash) was another form popularly used, and the name gave rise to the more familiar names Pierce and Pearce.

PILIP m. An Irish translation of Philip, ''lover of horses.'' Popularly used around the early to late Middle Ages, rarely encountered today.

PÓL m. (pole) An Irish form of Paul, which derives from a Latin word for "small."

PROINSÉAS f. (proon-shass) The Irish form of Frances, a name originating from the figure of Saint Francis of Assisi, whose name meant "little Frenchman." Proinnsias is another form, used for both Frances and the masculine form, Francis.

PROINSIAS/Proinnsias m. (proon-she-as or prun-she-as) Irish form of Francis, used with reverence toward Saint Francis of Assisi. Rather awkward-sounding and looking for contemporary tastes.

QUINLAN m. A use of the contemporary surname as a first name. Quinlan probably derives from Caoinleán (keen-lan), "of beautiful shape," a name used in the early period. Quinlevan and Quilan are related forms.

QUINN f. & m. The surname used as a first name, usually found in the United States, where it has been applied to both girls and boys. The source for this name is probably the old name Conn, "sense, intelligence," but as an Anglicized form of a surname, may as likely have come from a similar-sounding name like Cainneach/Canice, "pleasant person." Quinn is a commonly encountered surname in Ireland, especially in the north.

RAGHNAILT f. (rain-ilt) This name is a feminine form of Randal, "mighty power," a name brought to Ireland by the Vikings. The name became popular in the later Middle Ages and was Latinized as Regina.

RAICHBHE f. (rayv-a) A name without a clear meaning, borne by the sister of Saint Kieron of Clanmacnoise. Raveh is one possible Anglicized form.

RANDAL m. "mighty power" or "ruler's advice." The Vikings introduced this name, which was rendered as Raghnall (ran-ill or rain-ill) in Irish. The name proved popular by the eleventh century and was borne by a king of Waterford. It was well-used in the west and north of the country, and not surprisingly, occurs frequently in Scotland.

RATHNAIT f. (ron-it) From *rath,* "grace, prosperity." Saint Rathnait is a patron saint of Kilraghts, in County Antrim. Ronit is the Anglicized spelling, Renny is a pet form.

REDMOND m. This is the popular Irish form of Raymond, "counsel, protection," a name with Germanic origins. In Irish it was written Reamonn (ray-mon) and proved popular from late medieval times onward. Redmond O'Hanlon was a notorious highwayman and extortionist who preyed on Anglo settlers in the north and east of the country during the seventeenth century.

RHONA/Rona f. The origin of this name is uncertain, but it could derive from the masculine name Ronan, or from the feminine name Raghnailt. Records of usage begin as late as the nineteenth century in Scotland.

RICHAEL f. (reech-il or ri-chale) Perhaps containing the element *rí,* "king." A little-used, distinctly Irish name, despite the similarity to Rachel. In ecclesiastical lore, Richael was—what else—a virgin saint.

RILEY f. & m. Use of the contemporary surname, which usually occurs as Reilly, as a first name. From the Irish O Raghaillaigh, possibly "valiant." Principally found in the United States, Reilly, Rylee, and Ryley are also used.

RÍOFACH/Ríomhthach f. (reeve-ach) Ríofach was a sister of Saint Colman of Cloyne, and one of the five daughters of Lenine who were patronesses of Killiney, which name derives from Cill Inghean Léinín (kill ing-in layneen), "church of the daughters of Lenine."

RÍONA f. (ree-ona) From Ríonach, "queenly." Not surprisingly, the name has been translated as Regina, a name with the same meaning. Ríona was the maternal ancestor of many of the great Irish family lines. Two saints of record have borne the name. Sometimes used as a shortened form for Catriona.

RIORDAN m. (rear-don) From an early Irish name, Ríoghbhardáin (ree-vard-awn), "royal poet." A name that began as a profession, used then as a first, and finally as a last name. The bard was an important figure in any royal household, with responsibilities for historical accuracy, legal judgment, and artistic composition. Most usually found as a surname in Ireland today, in the United States and Canada it has been used, along with Rearden, as a first name.

RISTÉARD m. (rish-taird) An Irish form of Richard, "strong ruler." The name was brought to Ireland by Norman and Anglo-Norman settlers. Ristéard derives from the French form of the name, Richard, with a soft *ch* sound. The old English form, Ricard, with a hard *c,* was translated in Irish as Riocard (rick-ord). Both names found use in the Middle and late Middle Ages. Risderd (rish-dard) is a form peculiar to the Waterford region.

ROBUCK m. An unusual name, probably related to Robert, that occurs in the logs of the seventeenth-century Kinvan family of Galway.

RODEN m. (row-den) From the Irish *rod,* "strong." Usually found as a surname, this name has been used in the United States as a first name.

RODHLANN m. (row-lan) An Irish form of the Germanic-originated name Roland, "famous land."

ROIBEARD m. (row-beard or rib-eard) The Irish form of Robert, "bright fame." Introduced by the Normans, a number of forms have flourished including Ribeard, Ribeart, Riobárt, and Ribirt. The pet form of Robert, Robin, is Roibín or Roibean (rib-een or row-bin).

ROSS m. From a word meaning "headland." The name occurs in legend from early times on. Ross the Red was the legendary founder of the Red Branch, the sentinels of Ulster. Also taking the forms Rossa and Rosa, Ross has been steadily used from early times onward. All forms are currently used in Ireland today.

ROURKE/Roark/Rorke m. (ru-ark) From the old Irish Ruarc, a name thought to contain the element *arg,* "a hero, a champion." From it we get the contemporary surname O'Rourke.

RUMHANN/Rumann m. (ruv-an) An early name whose most distinguished bearer was the eighth-century poet Rumann Mac Colmáin (col-mawn) of Trim.

RYAN m. From Rían (ree-an), thought to be either a diminutive of *rí,* "king," hence "little king," or simply to imply "of royalty." Rarely used in Ireland except as a surname, Ryan has become very popular in the United States, Britain, and Australia, placing in the top twenty for some years now.

SADHBH/Sive f. (syve) Thought to mean "goodness" or "sweetness." In myth, Sadhbh was the mother of Oisín, a beautiful woman who was changed into a deer by a sorcerer. The name occurs in early records but became very popular in later medieval times. Several queens bore the name, as well as the daughters of regents Madhbh of Connacht and high king Brian Boru. Sadhbh, daughter of Conn Cétchathach ("of the hundred battles"), was recorded at the top of a list of the four "best women in Ireland who ever lay with a man." The name was Anglicized in the past as Sarah, Sabia, and Sophia. Sive is the current Anglicized form.

SAOIRBHREATHACH m. (sare-vra-huch) "noble of judgment." A name that occurs in the Middle Ages and well-used by certain families throughout that era including the MacCarthys and the MacEgans. Inevitably Anglicized as Justin, a name that has been consistently used in Ireland while out of favor elsewhere.

SAOIRSE f. (sare-sha) "freedom." A contemporary use of the word as a first name.

SAORLA/Saorlaith f. (sare-la) "noble princess." An early name, rarely recorded but ripe, one would think, for contemporary usage.

SARAID f. (sar-it or sar-ee) From *sar,* "best, noble." Saraid was another daughter of Conn Cétchatach, and through marriage, is maternal ancestor of the kings of Scotland. The name was Anglicized as Sarah.

SCOTT/Scot m. The use of the surname, meaning "a Scot," as a first name. Scotland is named for a tribe of settlers, the Scotti, who came there from Ireland. Indeed, the term *Scott,* at an early time, was used to describe the inhabitants of Ireland. The name came into general use as a first name in the twentieth century, especially in Britain and the United States, rising to a peak of popularity in the 1970s and, though currently fading, shows great staying power.

SCULLY m. Use of the contemporary surname as a first name. From O Scolaidhe and O Scolaighe, possibly meaning "descendant of the scholar" or "descendant of the town crier."

SÉADNA m. (shay-na) Possibly the name of a god, with a meaning like "traveler, wayfarer." Well-used in the early period, some thirteen saints are said to have borne the name. It was Anglicized as Sidney.

SÉAFRAID m. (sha-fraid) This is an Irish form of Geoffrey, a popular name introduced by the Anglo-Normans. Germanic in origin, the latter part of the name means "peace," but it is uncertain what the former part derives from, possibly from a term meaning "governor" or perhaps a development from the name Godfrey, "God's peace." The name accumulated a number of forms in Irish, being rendered also as Séathrún (shah-roon). Séafra, Siofraidh, Séafraidh, Siothrún, Searthún, Séartha, and Séarthra were all used. Sheary and Sheron are Anglicized forms. Séathrún Ceitinn (Geoffrey Keating) was a seventeenth-century historian who wrote a famous history of Ireland.

SÉAMAS/Seamus m. (shay-mus) An Irish form of James, "a supplanter, he who takes by the heel." The name was well-used, assuming many spellings and variations including Seumas, Séumus, Séamus, and the phonetic spelling Shamus. Pet forms used are Shay, Séimí (shay-me), Siomaidh (shu-me), Siomaidh (shee-me), and Simidh (shimmy), as well as Séamuisín (shay-museen) and Siomataigh (shim-atee). The name is still in common use in Ireland.

SEAN m. (shawn) An Irish form of John, "the Lord is gracious," which derives from the French form, Jean. The name was introduced by the Normans in the medieval period and was adopted by the Irish soon afterward. Contemporary Irish renders the name Seán, but Seón and Seaghán are other forms found. Pet forms are Seánín (shawn-een), Seónín (show-neen) and Seantaigh (shawn-tee). The phonetic spellings Shawn and Shaun have become very popular in Britain and the United States, where, along with Sean, they have been used also as girls' names. DeShawn and Shaughan are further U.S. elaborations used as male names. In Canada and the United States, feminine forms connected to this name have abounded. Shawna, Shauna, Shawnna, Shaune, Shauneen, and Shawndelle are examples.

SEARC f. (shark) "love, affection." A name borne by an early saint of Meath. Simple, with an attractive meaning, but with associations that are perhaps too daunting for contemporary use.

SÉARLAIT f. (shear-lat) The Irish form of Charlotte, probably originating in the eighteenth or nineteenth centuries. Charlotte is a feminine form of Charles.

SÉARLAS/Séarlus m. (shearl-us) The Irish form of Charles, a name with Germanic origins meaning "a man." Adopted in Ireland around about the eighteenth century.

SENAN/Seanán m. (senan or shan-awn) An early name, from *sen* or *sean*, "old, wise." The name was used more often as a title of respect to begin with, then developed into a first name. Saint Senan was a sixth-century saint who founded a monastery on Scattery Island, off the coast of Clare. Anglicized forms include Sinon, Sinan, and Synon.

SEOIRSE m. (shor-sha) An Irish form for the name George, which derives from the Greek word for "farmer." Used in Ireland only since the eighteenth century, when in England there was a succession of monarchs by the name George.

SEOSAIMHÍN f. (sho-saffeen) The Irish form of Josephine, a name with French origins; a feminine form of the Hebraic name Joseph.

SEOSAMH f. (sho-saff) The Irish form of Joseph, from the Hebrew name, "Jehovah shall add (another son)." The name also was rendered as Ióseph (yo-sef), and Seosap, Seosaph, and Iósep are variant forms.

SHANE m. This is another form of the name Sean, an Irish form of John. Shane was the popular form in Ulster and is widely used there with reference to the sixteenth-century patriot Shane O'Neill, whose forces successfully overcame those of the English monarch Elizabeth I, at Tyrone. The name was popularly adopted in the United States and Australia in the twentieth century and has been used for both girls and boys since. Shain and Shayne are variants.

SHANNA f. This is a modern American name, which likely derives from names such as Shannon that deploy the Irish phonetic device *shan-* at the beginning. Some sources suggest that Shanna is a shortened form of Shannon, which came into use as early as the 1940s. In the 1980s, an intensive use of this prefix in girls' names produced a vast range of related forms, as well as propelling the more traditional Shannon back up the list of favorites. Shannagh, Shannah, Shana, Shanae, Shanay, Shanell, Shanegua, Shanetta, Shanette, Shanika, Shanisha, Shante, and Shanice are some of the forms that evolved.

SHANNON f. The name of Ireland's longest river and probably a form of the name of an early Celtic divinity. From the root *sen*, or *Sean* (shan), "old," with a meaning like "old one." Rarely used as a first name in Ireland, Shannon was popularly being used by immigrant families in the United States, Canada, and Australia as early as the 1930s. The name began a slow ascendancy to broad popularity, occasionally being used as a boy's name, culminating in the 1970s, when it entered the top thirty list for girls' names and then exploded into myriad distinctive forms in the 1980s. The name has begun a slow decline in popularity in the United States, though it still places in the top fifty, but recently it has come on strongly in Britain, where it had been used more sparingly, showing in the top twenty favorites for 1996. Shannyn, Channon, and Shanyn are variant spellings, with the forms Shannen and Shanon also being used for boys.

SHEEDY m. Principally found as a surname today, Sheedy comes from the Irish Síoda, possibly meaning "silk."

SHERIDAN m. From Sirideán, the surname used as a first name. The meaning "eternal treasure," from the words *síor* and *dán,* has been proposed. Sheridon is another form.

SIBÉAL f. (shib-ale) This is an Irish form of Isabel or Isobel, the Spanish forms for Elizabeth. Iseabeál (isha-bale) is another Irish form of the name. Sibby is a pet form.

SÍNE f. (sheena) This is an Irish form of Jane, deriving from the French form Jeanne. Sheena is the more popular Scottish form of the name. Shena and Shenagh are also used.

SINEAD/Sinéad f. (shin-ade) An Irish form of the name Jane, or more properly, Janet, which are feminine forms derived from John. John was hugely popular as a man's name from the Middle Ages on, and Christians throughout Europe developed feminine versions. The French forms Jeanne, Jehanne, and Jeanette became in Ireland variously Síne, Siobhan, and Sinéad. Despite this, Sinéad was more frequently retranslated into alternative names such as Judith, Johanna, Hannah, Susanna, Judy, and Julia. The name is presently popular in Ireland, and has become more familiar internationally in the past twenty years. Sinéidín (shin-aideen) is a pet form.

SIOBHAN f. (shiv-aun) Another Irish feminine form derived from John. This name is probably a form of the French Jehanne, which in turn corresponds with the English form Joan. Siobhan has been used popularly in Ireland since its introduction in about the twelfth century. The old form was written Sibán or Siubhán, Siubhánín (shiv-au-neen) used as a pet form. The adoption of the name in other English-speaking countries has resulted in a wide range of spellings; principally, in the United States, Shavon and Shavonne. Other forms found include Shavaun, Shavonn, Shivonne, Shevan, Shivaun, Shevaun, Chavon, Chevonne, and Chivon. In the past, the name was translated in English into a wide variety of names that are unconnected, including Susan, Judith, Judy, Hannah, Julia, Nonie, and Jude.

SÍOMHA f. (sheeva) An old name that derives from *síth*, "peace." The name was borne by an eighth-century abbess of Clonburren. Employing contemporary conventions, it is possible that the name could be rendered Síobha, making it look more like the familiar Siobhan. Seeva is a possible Anglicization.

SLANY f. (slain-ey) This is an Anglicized form of the Irish name Sláine (slaw-nya), which is a word meaning "health." Sláine was used since the Middle Ages as a girl's name, though is rarely encountered today.

SOCHLA f. (such-la) "well-reputed, renowned." An early name recorded as that borne by the mothers of two saints, Feichín and Molua.

SORLEY m. From the Irish Somhairle (so-urla), which is an adaptation of an old Norse name meaning "summer wanderer." In Ireland, it came to refer to a Viking in general, as it was during the summertime, when the sea crossing was less hazardous, that the Vikings would sail south, raiding the coastlines of Scotland and Ireland.

SUANACH f. (sua-noch) "drowsy." The name occurs in legend as that of the sister of Finn Mac Cool, mother of the warrior Fiachra.

SWEENEY m. This name derives from the early Irish form Suibhne (swiv-neh). Suibhne was a well-used name, borne by kings and saints. Suibhne Gelt, or Mad Sweeney, is probably the most famous bearer of the name. He was a legendary seventh-century king who was sent mad by a curse inflicted by Saint Ronan. He appears in stories thereafter as a wild, wandering birdman and is invoked in later writings by W. B. Yeats and Flann O'Brien. The contemporary surname Sweeney derives from this source.

TADGH m. (ti-gue) "a poet." An old Irish name with records of use by kings and princes. Brian Boru's son held the name. Tadgh survived in use through the Middle Ages and down to modern times, when it was used as a term for "everyman," much like Jack in England. In the north, the name was Anglicized as Teague or Taig, names that are still used as deprecating terms for a Catholic. The form Teigue also occurs, but Tad is the most popularly found spelling in the United States. Translations that have been used for this name are Thaddeus, Theophilus, and Theodosius, though Timothy is most commonly used as an equivalent today. Tadleigh (tad-lee), Tadghán (tie-gawn), Taidhgín (tie-geen), and Thad are pet forms.

TAILLTE f. (tal-te) An early name that occurs in legend. One Taillte was the nurse of Lug Lámfhota, and another was the wife of Eochaidh, the last king of the legendary Fir Bolg, the aboriginals of Ireland.

TALLULA f. From the Irish Tuilelaith (twil-ay-la), "lady of abundance, abundance of sovereignty." The name was borne by two sainted abbesses of the eighth and ninth centuries. Twilleliah was the form favored in the seventeenth century. The actress Tallulah Bankhead, this century's most famous bearer of the name, shows another form, though her name may originate from the Native American place name, the Tallulah Falls in Georgia. Certainly a name with great potential in the coming millennium.

TARA f. (tar-ah) This is a name taken from the Irish place name Teamhair (towr), in county Meath. In legend, Teamhair takes its name from the wife of an early chieftain, but ruins found at Tara date back as far as 2000 B.C., predating the original sources of this legend. By 500 B.C., the site had become the central focus of royal and religious power in Ireland. The name has been interpreted to mean "eminence, elevated place." Through Margaret Mitchell's novel and the subsequent film, *Gone With the Wind*, the name has become familiar internationally in the twentieth century, and it has been used as a name for boys as well as girls. Popular in Ireland today, it is well-used in Canada and the United States, where the forms Tarrah, Tarra, Tarah, and Terra occur.

TEABÓID/Tiobóid m. (ta-boyd or ti-boyd) These are Irish forms of the Germanic name Theobald, which is composed of elements meaning "people" and "bold." Early pronunciation of Theobald across Europe was frequently Tibalt, and it is possible that this yielded the Irish form, which originated with the coming of the Normans. It was well-used by the prominent Butler family and was the name the pirate queen Grace O'Malley gave to her son. Theobald Wolfe Tone (1763–1798) was a distinguished Irish patriot, which helped to preserve the use of these names in Ireland.

TEFFIA f. This is the use of the place name—Teffia in County Longford—as a first name. Teffia gets its name from the Irish Teaffa (chaff-a), which indeed, was a name originally used by a lady associated with the site.

TIERNAN/Tiarnán/Tiárnán m. (tear-nen or tear-nawn) From *tigern* (tearn), "lord, chief." Tiernan was a name well-used in the early period, appropriately enough by chieftains, kings, and princes. There is a record of an early saint who bore the name. Tiarnan O'Ruairc, the warlike king of Breifne during the twelfth century, is one of the best-known bearers of the name.

TIERNEY f. & m. From the Irish name Tiernach, which comes from the same root as Tiernan, *tigern*, meaning "lord, chief." Several saints of record bore the name. This is the source of the contemporary surname, Tierney, which has been used in the United States as a girl's name. Tierna and Tiarna are other feminine forms found.

TÓLA m. (tow-la) "abundance, flood." A name borne by an early saint. To a contemporary ear, this name might seem more suitable for a girl.

TOMALTACH m. (tum-al-tach) An early name from the west, traditionally used by a group of families out of Connacht, including the MacDonaghs, Geraghtys, Mulrooneys, and O'Connors. Tomaltagh and Tumelty are variant forms.

TOMÁS m. (tom-aws) This is the Irish form of the biblical name Thomas, which means "twin." Originally used among the clergy, it was popularized in Ireland by the Anglo-Normans, who used it with reverence toward Saint Thomas à Becket (1118–1170). Tomaisín (tomas-een) is a pet form.

TREASA f. (trass-a) This name likely derives from the use of the name Treise, "strength." Recently, it has been used as an Irish form of Theresa, a name popular in Ireland on account of the inspirational figures Saint Theresa of Avila (1515–1582), and Saint Theresa of Lisieux (1873–1897).

TUATHAL m. (tua-hal) "ruler of the people." As befitting, the name was borne by many early kings and champions. Tuathal Teachtmar (chacht-var), "possessing wealth," is a legendary king said to have led the Gaels into Ireland. Toal and Tully are Anglicized forms.

TUATHLA f. (tua-la) A feminine form of Tuathal, which gives the attractive interpretation, "princess of the people." Tuathla was an eighth-century queen of Leinster.

TURLOUGH m. (tur-loch) Previously believed to have been connected with the name of the Norse god Thor, this name is now thought to be indigenous to Ireland, and to mean "instigator, abettor." Though not widely employed in the early period, it became popular during the Middle Ages after a slew of celebrated kings adopted the name in the eleventh and twelfth centuries. Turlough O'Connor was king of Connacht and high king of Ireland. Tarla and Tarlach are variant forms. As well as being translated as Charles, the name was translated as Terence and Terry, two names that have come to be strongly associated with Ireland.

ULICK m. (yoo-lich) From the Irish Uilleóg (ill-eogue), which is itself a diminutive of Uilliam, the Irish form for William. Anglicized sometimes as Ulysses.

ULTAN m. (ult-in) Meaning "an Ulsterman." A relatively common name in the early period, borne by some eighteen saints of record, the most famous of whom, Saint Ultan of Ardbraccan from the seventh century, is the patron saint of Ireland's children.

UNA f. (oon-a) A well-used name from early times onward. Una was the mother of Conn of the Hundred Battles. Another Una was claimed as the fairy patroness of the O'Carroll family. Una MacDermott is the seventeenth-century subject of the tragic lyric, "Una Bhán" ("Fair Una"). In the past, the name was Anglicized as Winnifrid, Winny, Agnes, and Unity, and has contemporary Anglicized spellings Oona and Oonagh.

USNA m. Usna was, in legend, an Ulster chieftain, father to Naoise, Ainle, and Ardan, the brothers treacherously slain by Conchobhar Mac Nessa over the love of Deirdre.

Calendar

The following calendar is drawn from Father Patrick Woulfe's calendar of saints' feast days, originally published in his *Irish Names for Children* in 1923. His principal source was *The Martyrology of Donegal*. Father Woulfe's calendar included quite a few more names than are presented here, but the impression should be clear that there exist rather more Irish saints of record than there are days in the year (though not every day has its Irish saint). Father Woulfe urged parents to consider adopting a name for their children from this calendar, especially if the child's birthday fell on a day devoted to a particular saint. "In such cases," he offered, "the child is said to have 'brought its name with it.' " It is quite possible, perusing some of the names presented here, that your child would argue strongly against this viewpoint. But there may be some merit in this exercise, if not at least a deal of curiosity. Alas, it is often the case that there is precious little known about the individual saints commemorated here.

Reviewing these names, one is struck with the frequent occurrence of the same group of names and, indeed, the range presented is quite narrow, contrasted with the variety recorded elsewhere in this book. It is likely that certain names were favored by the clergy, many of whom may have graduated to sainthood. Parents interested in playing Father Woulfe's game take note; if you favor the names Colman, Comyn, or Cronan, you are in luck.

January

	· 1 · Fainche Colman Aodhán Fintan Oisín	· 2 · Mannix
· 3 · Killian Fintan	· 4 · Aodh Feenat	· 5 · Kieran
· 6 · Dermot Mona	· 7 · Cronan Donnán Evin	· 8 · Fionán Killian
· 9 · Faolán Kieran Brendan	· 10 · Dermot	· 11 · Sweeney Ronan Fáilbhe

· 12 ·	· 13 ·	· 14 ·
Comyn Conan	Mannix Colman Ronan	Flann
· 15 ·	· 16 ·	· 17 ·
Ide	Dermot Maeliosa Killian	Ultan
· 19 ·	· 20 ·	· 21 ·
Fachtna Sweeney	Feichín Cronan Aengus Fergus	Flann Fainche
· 22 ·	· 23 ·	· 25 ·
Colman Lonán	Lucan Canice	Aodh
· 26 ·	· 27 ·	· 28 ·
Eirnín	Lucan	Meallán
· 29 ·	· 30 ·	· 31 ·
Bláth Cronan	Alby Cronan	Aodhán Canice

February

· 1 · Brigid	· 2 · Colman	· 3 · Colman Keelin
· 4 · Loman Kieran	· 5 · Fineen	· 6 · Colm
· 7 · Aodh Meallán Colman Loman Fintan Lonán	· 8 · Colman Fiachra Fáilbhe	· 9 · Ronan Colman

· 11 ·	· 12 ·	· 13 ·
Finnian Gobnet Dubhán	Siadhal Lughaidh Fionán Cronan Comyn Aodhán	Conan Fionán
· 14 ·	· 15 ·	· 16 ·
Mannix	Bearach Fergus	Aodh Aengus
· 17 ·	· 18 ·	· 19 ·
Fintan Cormac	Aengus Colman	Feichín Oran
· 20 ·	· 21 ·	· 22 ·
Cronan	Fintan Colman Cronan	Feichín
· 23 ·	· 24 ·	· 25 ·
Eirnín	Comyn Kieran	Keenan
· 26 ·	· 27 ·	· 28 ·
Cronan Becan Eithne	Comgan	Eirnín

March

· 1 · Senan Colm	· 2 · Lugaidh Conall Cuan Finnian

· 3 · Conall Killian Fachtna	· 5 · Kieran Carthach	· 6 · Cairbre Oran Brigid
· 8 · Senan Kieran Siadhal Cronan Conan	· 9 · Brigid Lughaidh Proinnseas Séadna	· 10 · Séadna Fáilbhe Colman
· 11 · Aengus	· 12 · Killian	· 14 · Ultan Flannán

· 15 ·	· 16 ·	· 17 ·
Eoghan	Aodhán Fionán	Patrick Becan
· 18 ·	**· 20 ·**	**· 21 ·**
Conall Comyn	Aodhán Conan	Éanna
· 22 ·	**· 23 ·**	**· 24 ·**
Fáilbhe	Fergus Mannix Ciannait	Lughaidh
· 26 ·	**· 27 ·**	**· 28 ·**
Carthach Cormac Garvan Killian	Fintan	Conall
· 29 ·	**· 30 ·**	**· 31 ·**
Fergus Aodhán Eithne	Fergus Colman	Fáolan

April

· 1 · Kelly Aodhán	· 2 · Conall	· 3 · Comyn
· 4 · Ultan Colman	· 5 · Becan	· 7 · Senan Fionán Aodh
· 8 · Ronan Fáilbhe Tiernan Aodhán	· 9 · Colman Senan	· 10 · Bercan Killian

· 11 ·	· 12 ·	· 14 ·
Aodh	Eirnín	Killian
Senan		Colman
· 15 ·	· 16 ·	· 17 ·
Rúadhán	Ultan	Donnán Garvan
	Fáilbhe	Eochaidh
		Lughaidh
· 18 ·	· 20 ·	· 21 ·
Eoghan	Flann	Bearach
Laisrean	Donnán	
	Fáilbhe	
· 22 ·	· 24 ·	· 26 ·
Callaghan	Dermot	Becan Senan
		Cronan Conan
		Donal
· 27 ·	· 28 ·	· 30 ·
Ultan	Cronan	Ronan
	Sweeney	Kieran

May

	· 1 · Ultan Oisín Mannix Ronan	· 2 · Fiachra Colman
· 3 · Cairbre	· 4 · Aodh Cronan	· 5 · Faolán Senan
· 6 · Colman	· 7 · Bercan	· 8 · Comyn Brendan Oran
· 10 · Cole Aodh Cathal	· 12 · Eirnín	· 14 · Carthach Garvan

· 15 ·	· 16 ·	· 17 ·
Murry Colman Comyn Davnit Colm	Brendan Oran	Finnian
· 18 ·	· 19 ·	· 20 ·
Bran Colman Brassal	Kieran Comyn Richael	Colman
· 21 ·	· 22 ·	· 23 ·
Colman Finbar Comyn Ronan Brigid	Conall Ronan	Criofan Comyn
· 24 ·	· 25 ·	· 26 ·
Ultan Bercan Colman	Donnagh	Becan Colman
· 27 ·	· 28 ·	· 31 ·
Killian	Faolán Eoghan	Eoghan Eirnín

June

	· 1 · Cronan Comyn Colman	· 2 · Aodhán Senan
· 3 · Kevin	· 4 · Colm Eirnín Colman	· 5 · Bercan
· 6 · Jarleth Faolán Colman Lonán	· 7 · Colm	· 9 · Colm
· 10 · Bearach	· 12 · Gillespie Cronan	· 13 · Davnit

· 14 ·	· 15 ·	· 16 ·
Kieran	Colman	Séadna Colman
· 17 ·	· 18 ·	· 19 ·
Colman Aodhán	Colman	Colman
· 20 ·	· 21 ·	· 22 ·
Faolán	Sweeney Dermot	Cronan Sweeney
· 23 ·	· 24 ·	· 26 ·
Faolán	Cormac	Colman
· 27 ·	· 28 ·	· 30 ·
Aodh	Eirnín	Caolán Fáilbhe

July

· 1 ·	· 3 ·	· 4 ·
Comyn Eirnín Conan Ultan	Killian Maolmhuire Ultan	Finbar
· 5 ·	· 6 ·	· 8 ·
Etain Fergus Ultan	Blinne Eithne	Dermot Tadgh Killian Colman
· 9 ·	· 10 ·	· 11 ·
Garvan	Cuan Ultan Aodh Senan	Fáilbhe Lonán Colman

· 12 · Colman Ultan	· 13 · Fintan Ultan Eirnín	· 14 · Colman
· 15 · Colman Ronan	· 17 · Flann	· 18 · Fintan Cronan Fáilbhe Kelly
· 19 · Oisín Aodhán Colman Fergus Kieran	· 20 · Fáilbhe	· 22 · Oisín Colman
· 24 · Declan Cole Cronan	· 25 · Colman Fiachra Finbar Caolán Neasán	· 27 · Brendan
· 28 · Cole	· 29 · Comyn Caolán	· 31 · Colman

August

		· 1 · Colm Fáilbhe
· 2 · Lonán Feichín Comgan	· 3 · Feidhlimid Aodhán	· 5 · Colman Eirnín Rathnait
· 6 · Lughaidh	· 7 · Cronan Killian Aodhán Senan	· 8 · Colman
· 9 · Ultan Colman Feidhlimid Kieran	· 10 · Comyn	· 11 · Attracta Donnán

· 12 ·	· 13 ·	· 14 ·
Iomhar Brigid	Laisrean Murry	Fachtna Comyn
· 15 ·	· 16 ·	· 17 ·
Aodh Colman	Conan	Becan Senan
· 18 ·	· 22 ·	· 23 ·
Eirnín Oran Colman Ronan	Comyn	Eoghan
· 24 ·	· 26 ·	· 27 ·
Faolán	Cole Faolán	Aodhán
· 28 ·	· 30 ·	· 31 ·
Feidhlimid	Fiachra Cronan	Aodhán Aodh Killian

September

		· 1 · Comyn Fáilbhe
· 2 · Senan Colm	· 3 · Colman	· 4 · Ultan Fáilbhe Comyn Fiachra Cole Senan Aodhán
· 6 · Colm Colman Ultan	· 8 · Fintan Fergus	· 9 · Kieran Finbar Conall
· 10 · Finnian Oran Finbar Fergus	· 11 · Colman	· 12 · Alby Colman

· 13 ·	· 14 ·	· 16 ·
Nevan	Cormac	Laisrean Senan Colman
· 17 ·	· 19 ·	· 20 ·
Comyn	Fintan	Aodhán
· 22 ·	· 23 ·	· 24 ·
Aodh Colm Colman	Adhamhnán	Callaghan
· 25 ·	· 26 ·	· 27 ·
Finbar Senan Caolán Colman	Colman	Finnian
· 28 ·	· 29 ·	· 30 ·
Fiachra Dermot	Neasán Cole Kieran Colman Colm	Lughaidh Brigid Faolán Senan Colman

October

		· 1 · Colm Fintan ·Colman
· 2 · Oran	· 4 · Colman Senan Fionán	· 6 · Lughaidh Colman Aodh
· 7 · Cole Kelly Colma	· 8 · Kieran	· 9 · Fintan Aodhán
· 10 · Fintan Senan	· 11 · Canice Loman	· 12 · Fiachra Aodhán Dermot Faolán

· 13 ·	· 14 ·	· 15 ·
Comgan	Colm	Cuan Cormac Colman
· 16 ·	· 18 ·	· 19 ·
Colman Colm Kevin Eoghan	Colman	Cronan Colman Faolán
· 20 ·	· 21 ·	· 22 ·
Aodhán Fintan Colman	Fintan Mannix	Killian
· 23 ·	· 24 ·	· 25 ·
Killian	Lonán Colman	Laisrean
· 26 ·	· 27 ·	· 28 ·
Oran	Oran Colman	Colman Sweeney Conan
· 29 ·	· 30 ·	· 31 ·
Colman Aodh Cuan Caolán	Colman Feidhlimid	Comyn Colman Faolán

November

· 1 ·	· 2 ·
Cairbre Colman Lonán Cronan Brendan Aodh	Aodhán Lughaidh Caoimhe

· 5 ·	· 6 ·	· 8 ·
Colman Flannán Faolán	Cronan Colman Aodhán Fintan	Colm

· 9 ·	· 10 ·	· 11 ·
Beanon Aodhnait Fintan	Aodh Comyn Kieran Fergus	Cairbre Cronan Dubhán

· 12 · Comyn Lonán Mannix Eirnín	**· 13 ·** Orna Eirnín	**· 14 ·** Lorcan Colman
· 16 · Fintan	**· 17 ·** Aengus	**· 18 ·** Ronan
· 21 · Colman Garvane Aodhán Comyn	**· 22 ·** Ultan Maeve	**· 24 ·** Colman Keenan Bercan
· 25 · Fergal	**· 27 ·** Brendan Feenat Keenan	**· 30 ·** Comyn

December

		· 1 · Neasán Brendan
· 2 · Mannix	· 3 · Colman	· 4 · Bercan Mannix
· 5 · Colman Senan	· 6 · Meallán Neasán Colman	· 8 · Brendan Fionán
· 10 · Colman	· 11 · Colm	· 12 · Finnian

· 13 ·	· 14 ·	· 15 ·
Brendan Colm Cormac	Cormac Colman Fintan Eirnín	Flann Colman Cronan
· 18 ·	· 20 ·	· 21 ·
Comyn Senan Ríona Colman Flannán Evin	Dermot Eoghan Feidhlimid	Flann
· 22 ·	· 23 ·	· 24 ·
Ultan Evin	Colman Ronan Eirnín Feidhlimid	Maolmhuire Comyn Senan
· 25 ·	· 26 ·	· 27 ·
Aodhán	Jarleth Comyn Laisreand	Fiach Colman
· 28 ·	· 29 ·	· 31 ·
Killian Feichín	Mannix	Éanna

Index of Names

Abaigeal, 68
Abaigh, 68
Abhlach, 38
Ádam, 68
Adamair, 21
Adamnan, 76
Ádhamh, 14, 68
Adhamhnán, 76
Adhamhnán, 149
Adomnán, 76
Áedán, 19–20
Aengus, 72, 76–77,
  133, 135, 136,
  153
Affraic, 77
Africa, 77
Ágata, 68
Ághmach, 46
Ághuistín, 69
Aibhílín, 77
Aibhistín, 69
Aichear, 46
Aidan, 19–20
Aidrian, 68
Aifric, 77
Aignéis, 68

Ailbe, 9, 72
Ailbhe, 9, 73
Ailchú, 26
Aileen, 77
Ailfrid, 68
Ailill, 77
Ailín, 68
Ailionóra, 69
Ailís, 68, 77
Ailíse, 68
Ailish, 77
Aimilíona, 68
Ainbheartach, 54
Aindréas, 69
Aindreas, 77
Aindrias, 69, 77
Aindriú, 69
Áine, 20, 60–61, 73
Ainéislis, 78
Ainfeach, 54
Ainfean, 54
Aingeal, 69, 77
Ainmire, 54
Ainníleas, 54
Aisling, 73, 78
Aislinn, 73, 78

Alana, 78
Alannah, 78
Alastar, 78
Alastrina, 78
Alastríona, 68, 78
Albany, 9
Alby, 9, 72–73,
  133, 148
Allana, 78
Almha, 73, 78
Aloysius, 46
Alsander, 68
Alva, 78
Amhalgaidh, 79
Amhlaoibh, 79
Anbhile, 38
Anéislis, 73
Aneslis, 73, 78
Anfudán, 54
Ánna, 69
Annraoi, 70
Ánnstas, 69
Anraí, 70
Aodh, 20, 73, 132–
  135, 138, 140,
  143–144,